RETHINK YOUR FINANCIAL HEALTH

SHARING THE MANUAL: FOUR LENSES TO
FINANCIAL HEALING AND WHOLENESS

aj uitvlugt

Rethink Your Financial Health
Copyright © 2023 by Amie Uitvlugt

Tellwell Talent
www.tellwell.ca

ISBN
978-0-2288-8691-4 (Hardcover)
978-0-2288-8690-7 (Paperback)
978-0-2288-8692-1 (eBook)

Dedication

This book is dedicated to my three beautiful children and my late husband. Our journey has been difficult; throughout it all my dear children, you have loved me unconditionally. I am forever grateful for your unwavering belief in me and endless compassion towards my trial and errors as I unlearn and relearn—I could not be prouder of each one of you for embarking on our life's journey as one tribe.

Without your passing, my beloved Bart, I would not have authored Rethink Your Financial Health. It was through the grief, suffering, and financial burdens of losing everything that I can give this book to others and bring about financial wholeness within me and our beautiful children.

May this book be a blessing to others.

A Journey Within

A woman able to check off every relationship status known to man: single, married, widowed, separated, divorced. I am an overachiever and a comedian. Through my journey, I crafted a money story that derailed my financial future. So I embarked on a journey to find meaning.

Having gone through this healing journey myself, I now bring you this book - Hey, here's my manual of what not to do, LMAO.

I bring you real stories, humour, and enlightenment to empower you to break through and become financially whole today.

In life, we have lenses through which we view the world:

- What we were told.
- What we learned.
- What we experienced.
- What we believe to be our truth.

Rethink Your Financial Health will help you dismantle your limiting beliefs about money, self, and your future.

A journey within to financial healing and wholeness is yours, shall we.......

Table of Contents

Preface

OUT OF THE FAST LANE 2022

I have been in this new house for two months now.
I miss the acreage, the massive pine trees,
Alana, Codie, Monika laughing outside the kitchen
window.
"Daddy's home!"

Alana has his piercing blue eyes,
Codie, his charm.
Little Miss Monie is mischievous like him;
she has my spunk and blonde hair:
the perfect blend of us.

On the way to Walmart with my gals, my Bluetooth
picks up the call:
"Ms. Uitvlugt
This is Constable Tim, are you in a safe location
Ma'am?"
This cannot be good.
I pull over, jump out of the car.
I do not want my girls to hear.

"Ma'am, I am so sorry, we are going to need you to come identify the body."

Bart's gone!
If I responded to his text yesterday, would he still be here?
My kids...

This is our new normal...
I am strong.
I will FAST TRACK through this.
I color-code my calendar, no whitespace—
cannot risk feeling.
Codie has hockey, he made the CAL travel team,
Alana—on the ice four days a week with Ringette.
Little Miss Monie—gymnastics, Mondays and Wednesdays
Sit in solitude at the rink? Not a chance!
I ran 10k instead.

When that stops working,
I dig into our savings:
A Disney cruise to St Maarten and the Bahamas,
a trip to Florida...
Seeing my kids' smile helps, a bit.

Driving to Ontario, I see a shiny, new, white Jeep,
top down, doors off:
I must have IT!
Cannot be... my account balance is zero!
I have to use my retirement money.

Up next, relationships.

Nope, next, moving on...
Ivan: we tried twice, such a great guy;
we could not make it work.
Fran won me with his adventurous spirit.
He is good to me and my kids.

Less than three years go by...
we are so disconnected.
Here I am, lost, unrecognizable.

Why does this keep happening?

I have been running so fast, numbing everything.
Bart's death was not my fault.
I need to slow down,
forgive myself,
and connect with my family.

Alana and I are doing a 5k run this morning.
This is my chance to open up:
"Alana. I really miss your dad."
"Me too, Mom."
Do you know what we did next?
We walked.
When I got home, I shared it with Codie and Monika; we cried.
It feels good to let them in.

The other day, my work friend Kyla and I were looking through Kijiji, for puppies.
"I need one, to get me through."
Hmmm... Molly, Anigo, Boe, Bella: I have done this before.

Another emotional purchase?
No.
I am choosing to feel my emotions and save for my future.

It is so good to slow down and let myself feel.
I am healing.

Everything has changed:
my finances,
my connection to my family,
ME.
I am whole.

Introduction

If you have not already guessed, I have taken my mess and it has become my message: pain to purpose—sharing the manual is what I like to say. The manual of what not to do, lol. After being widowed in 2013, I have come to realize things that I thought were common sense, are not so common. Especially, when it comes to money. I was a stay-at-home mom: three, beautiful kids ages nine, seven, and three. My husband was a plumber gas fitter; we had our own company and our sole purpose was for me to be able to stay home and raise our kids while he worked his bag off to set us up for our future. Repeatedly, I would hear the words, "just let me get us ahead and then I will slow down." Starting a business is no easy feat; it typically takes a good five years before things are on their way. We were in year seven when I had finally asked him to slow down, spend more time at home, and hire more guys. I was even planning to go back to work, to alleviate the pressure on him. On the outside looking in, it seems as if we had it all. This was far from the truth, as we had our struggles. Looking back now, Bart's identity was wrapped up in the business.

The weekend of his thirtieth birthday, he took a trip. We had a big fight about business, family, and balance and that something had to change. Had I known that would be our last conversation, I would have done things differently. Our world shattered in an instant. That is when the phone call came: he was gone. I was now in a very vulnerable position. I had to sell our acreage over the phone, as the banks did not cover the mortgage. He had held a small life insurance policy but had refused to apply for more because he was a smoker and wanted to quit first, to get the best rates. I packed up our dream home, that we had built less than two years earlier.

As I sat in my car at the end of the drive, with my three kids in the back seat, and watched the moving truck pull out onto the gravel road, I was paralyzed. I looked at the rear-view mirror and thought about what life was supposed to look like, as tears streamed down everyone's cheeks. I had yet to fully understand the magnitude of the situation.

I moved to a new city, with a dead husband, no job, no education, and no credit score or plan. I was experiencing ignorance and naiveté in the face of the "what ifs" that can happen in life. We did not plan for any of this. We simply worked hard—head down and ass up.

I remember sitting at the bank, staring at the teller, not understanding why my credit card was cancelled. Why, after all these years of banking, did I have no credit score? I was lost, confused, and terrified, as to how I was going to raise three kids. Everything of ours was joint, and my husband was the primary account holder. When he died, all the banking history, the credit score, it all went with him to the grave.

I took that summer off and lived off savings in hopes to help the kids and I find joy and happiness, again. I tried it all—living by the water, buying skateboards, paddle boards, taking trips, and camping. That summer ended, and we had made a dent in our savings, so it was time that I got a job. It was September, on the first day of school, and I dropped off the kids to head to the service desk at a local trailer company, for my first day of work. I had spent these last nine years as a stay-at-home mom and was not sure what working away from home was even like or if I could manage both roles. But I had no choice—we had to make this work.

At ten o'clock the phone rings and it is the school calling to tell me that my son is throwing up. I left work early to pick him up and bring him home. It was not the greatest start to a first day at a new job. We cuddled on the coach, and he seemed good. The next day it happened again. At this point I am apologizing to my new boss, trying to reassure him that my kids are usually not sick this often. This continued for the remainder of the week. My boss then tells me: "I'm sorry, this isn't working out."

Oh no! I was fired, for the first time ever. This rocked me. I was known as a diligent worker—dedicated, loyal, and punctual. What now? I picked my son up from school and we went home. He was bouncing off the walls; he wanted to go to the park and skateboard. I looked at him with tears in my eyes, "Dude, your mom just lost her job because you've been sick at school every day." His big eyes welled up with tears. "Mom, I just did not want you to die next. So, if I am home, then I know you are okay."

There is no manual on how to grieve and parent children at the same time. I had no idea the magnitude of the effect the loss of their father would have on the kids, when I decided to work right away. I decided to take two years off and live off our investments with the hope this would help the kids transition and ease them into the new normal of different schools, living without their dad, and their mom working away from home.

This was a big shift for them. If I am one hundred per cent honest, I do not remember much of the first year. I remember crying because I could not remember what I had done for my kids' birthdays. My dear friend reminded me that we had celebrated them, and I cried because I could not remember anything. She held me and said, "You were carried that year, my dear." I then realized that I was not ready to do it on my own yet: "God can continue to carry me." She laughed and said, "it does not work that way." (Insert big sigh.) We experienced difficulties, laughter, and tears, melt downs, and celebrations. I did anything I could, to bring smiles to their faces.

There were hard seasons that included words like, "Mom, I hate you, I wish it were you that died," and "no wonder why dad left," as well as kids who ran away from home—it was chaos. I wanted a normal life, one with vacations, new vehicles, a house to call home, kid's activities, and sports. All I wanted was meaning, purpose, happiness, security, and love. I wanted to be able to raise my kids to know that their dad loved them dearly, and that I was doing the best that I could. I wanted to show them that when life gives you lemons, you make lemonade.

We made a choice to start sharing our story after years of wallowing and faking it—and we did both. I teetered on that line for a while. Something needed to change; I went back to school to get my license in life insurance. I wanted people to plan, to be ready for life's unexpected detours, and alleviate the anguish that we went through. Money never brings them back, but it can help take the stress and pressure off financially. Money can give you time to heal, be there for your kids, and make informed financial decisions, at the right time, with the right guidance.

I learned that in this industry, advisors do not talk about the aftermath of a loved one's passing or the emotions that play a role in your money. That is when I decided to launch my own business: one that marries financial planning principles with the psychology of money. True wealth starts from within. This is a journey that I went on and now wish to bring to you, through this book- Rethink Your Financial Health.

I took a deeper dive into the emotions around money and the psychology behind our decisions when it comes to money. I learned about myself and my attachments to money throughout the years. What I learned took me on a financial healing journey, and I realized that my wounds from growing up—middle school, dating, losing a loved one, and starting over—have played a role in my financial decisions, both consciously and subconsciously. I did inner work on my identity as it was tied to many things, to starting again after a separation. The self-talk—lies I repeated to myself—was sabotaging my future. We all do it; it is about awareness and reprogramming. I have now started over twice, rebuilding, and working through my worthiness of abundance. If I can do it, so can you.

It is my intention to make this book simple to navigate and work through. Each chapter includes five components, an opening quote that I feel is relevant, followed by me sharing the manual with you. We then look through the lenses:

What were you told?

What did you learn?

What have you experienced?

What do you believe to be true?

This is followed by an exercise: the "Know, Believe, Do" model and Reader Reflections.

I hope you will complete the exercises after each chapter. By doing this work, you will be able to take back the power you may have lost throughout the years when it comes to your money. You are not alone in your journey. Others have gone before you, and I, my dear one, have shit the bed, so you do not have to! I have taken my failures and used them as opportunities to gain experience, to learn, and to bring you along with me for the lifelong adventure of healing and becoming financially whole. It is your turn to take this journey. Be prepared to have a completely different outlook on your finances when you are done.

How you read this book is your choice: cover-to-cover or by using the Financial Health Scorecard at the back of the book to jump into each chapter that speaks to the area that you want to develop and grow. Of course, I am going to suggest front-to-back, so you get all the juicy nuggets spread throughout this book. As the author, I encourage you to write within these pages, dog-tagging the ones that are relevant to you. If you saw the books I have read and my approach, it might send you into a panic attack. I circle, underline, highlight, scratch out, dog-tag, and bend. The more tattered and worn the book only shows how impactful it has been for you. Rethink Your Financial Health is meant to stretch you to live on the edge a little. Your goal throughout this book is to stay curious and lean in with possibility.

There is more to money than numbers, let me show you. Let us begin...

Chapter One: Why Financial Health Is Important

"Do the best you can until you know better, then when you know better, do better."

–Maya Angelou

The stats are out: 40 per cent of Canadians consider themselves financially unwell, and only 34 per cent of Americans are considered financially healthy.

Debt wreaks emotional havoc on our psyche. The financial strain affects all our lives: our families, relationships, our emotional, and mental wellbeing, our physical health, and not to mention, our careers and work performance. I know this firsthand.

Our basic needs are safety, food, water, and finances. Yes, when finances are not met or threatened, there is a natural stress response. Our ventral branch of vagal nerves is now engaged with our fight, flight, or freeze response. Among the adverse effects are low self-esteem, impaired cognitive functioning, and risk exposure. You cannot learn, remember, be attentive, or solve problems, when you are freaking out about money.

The additional risks of injury or illness as a result, are astronomical. Half a million Canadians miss work every week, due to mental health. Our finances play a role in our health and our wellness. It is time we aim for financial wholeness as part of our self-care.

Financial wholeness is a profound way of living out our money. This is when all aspects of your financial life work together for your greatest good, greatest benefit, and richest life. Financial wholeness starts within; it is achieved when we can self-regulate and work though the underlying problems. Recognize that our emotions are in the driver's seat to all our financial decisions.

We have hopes, dreams, fears, guilt, anxiety, shame and embarrassment regarding money. Money avoidance is real; we even have money trauma. However, we cannot sit back and be passive about our financial future—we must be active participants.

Throughout our lives we have each cultivated a money story. Understanding our money stories allows us to reflect on what is true and what is false. We have subconscious patterns that can leave us stuck and hinder our financial future, until we shed light on them and break them apart. Feelings about money are tied to identity, security, safety, upbringing, our first memories of money, society, partners, social media, and so much more. It is time we start thinking about our finances differently, to break apart our limiting beliefs and reach financial abundance.

I refer to lenses often in this book. Lenses are things we look through, which give us a certain perception—maybe you view money as a numbers game. I hope to challenge you to put on a different lens. In this book, the lens in which we see money is one of a healing journey, where we unpack patterns, and what is underneath them. There is always something underneath; I come from an extensive line of rug-sweepers, if you know what I mean.

Dismantling our limiting beliefs and the lies we believe about money, chiseling away at our money stories allows us to rebuild and rewire our neurological pathways, and release money behaviors that hinder our success. I have a model: Know, Believe, Do. When head knowledge becomes heart knowledge, we are able to live differently. It all happens simultaneously; you cannot do one without the others.

As we dive deeper into our own experiences, we can recognize where we have taken on different behaviors, habits, and belief systems that stem from our own life experiences, both good and bad. Think about what you were told. These could be words spoken with the best of intentions, however, throughout life, we interpret them to fit a narrative that we live out. A splendid example was shared with me just the other day, of a parent speaking to their young adult: "You just need enough to live." If we break that simple sentence down, there is a "lack-of" mindset here, that may limit us to only reaching for "enough". The belief that any "more" would be excessive or wasteful, is limiting. Words have power. Our minds are phenomenal machines—we can change the original narrative or intent.

What we learned about money is another filter that needs our attention. Many areas contribute to our learning, including our parents, schools, communities, the world, and social media. Everyone has an opinion regarding finances and money, and we take on other peoples' beliefs or narratives about money at an early age. Here is a typical example: "Money is the root of all evil." Can you relate to hearing this one? Hearing something repetitively as a kid has a lasting impact on how you live out money. We are "peeling back the onion" to find truth and ultimately develop an abundant, thriving, financial mindset.

Experiences have a way of solidifying a narrative we may already have been exposed to, or even build a new one. We have feelings, emotions, and memories that can be activated subconsciously. A gentleman shared this example with me and I could not help but laugh: A boy grew up in a home where money was scarce. There was a "lack-of" mentality and they lived paycheck-to-paycheck. The family often referred to people with money as "RB's" (Rich Bastards, for short). Think about this for a second, as this example displays multiple lenses: first, what the boy was told, and then, what he learned by watching family interactions. In later years, this young man, who still believed that people with money are "Rich Bastards", had an experience at a store in which the interactions between a male customer and staff, were unpleasant. The rude man left in his Porsche. This has just solidified the young man's beliefs that rich people are bastards. He may very well live out his financial life in such a way as to never be classified as "having money"—because, in his mind, it comes with a harmful connotation.

Change is hard when our heads and hearts are not connected. Many of us have blocks that hinder our financial futures. This journey will help you remove the blocks that stop you from having it all.

Financial freedom, wellness, and whole-life excellence, await!

I want to equip you all to kick ass and increase your financial health! With each chapter, we will first go through the "Know, Believe, Do" model, and then make time for reflection. With reflection comes change and the ability to apply new concepts.

KNOW: Head knowledge.

BELIEVE: Heart understanding.

DO: Head and heart work together to make change.

READER REFLECTIONS

Let's start with writing out your intention for getting and reading this book. What is the end goal for you?

Chapter Two: Money Mindset is a Hoax

"Your bad attitude is like a flat tire, and it won't get you anywhere till you change it."

–Unknown

Does this make you laugh? I chuckled because there is so much truth to it.

We often hear about "money mindset;" it is good to be aware of and honestly, it can feel like a hoax, too. According to Dave Ramsey, the definition of money mindset is "A unique set of beliefs and your attitude about money." Money mindset drives our decisions about saving, spending, and navigating our finances. (Keep in mind I have read his books and agree with his work).

On another site, you can find "five simple steps to shift your money mindset.", Sounds pretty contradictory, so which is it? Hard work or five simple steps and bingo, Bob's your uncle! You are suddenly financially healthy. Let us be honest, if that were the case, the world would not be in the state it is today With the financial health statistics as high as they are for Canadians and Americans, this is no quick fix. Sorry to be a Debbie Downer but I am a realist and I call it how I see it. I tried all the quick fixes to get my finances in order, and none of them stuck. It is not for lack of grit, let me tell you—this gal has plenty of that!

Don't get me wrong—I think and know that there is useful content out there with excellent tips and tricks that, when implemented, can bring about change. The problem I have experienced, is that the "quick fix" is typically short-lived. I will explain, using the lenses.

The root of the issue is that frequently, our money patterns and beliefs do not even stem from money! Remember how I talked about the lenses? Yes, I am bringing them back. We can use these same lenses for other areas within our lives, as well.

These lenses: what we were told, learned, and experienced, contribute to formulating our belief system.

The "what we are told" lens refers to words that have been spoken over us, words we have overheard, and things we hear.

What we learned could be things we have seen demonstrated, teachings at school, things our parents taught us, conversations we overheard, lessons we learned from television, social media, and the world around us.

The lens of experience includes our five senses, what has happened to us over the course of our life, as well as others close to us.

Through these lenses we begin to craft our identity, self-worth, values, insecurities, and what we determine we deserve. We take on our belief systems as if they are our truth when they are not. Are you following me?

From childhood, we create a story, or narrative, and live it out. We seek to justify our beliefs, which are subconscious behaviors that keep us stuck. No one is immune to this. I, too, need to be self-aware and I do a regular inventory to see if I have fallen into old patterns and behaviors.

The good news is, once we build, create, and nurture these new, healthy neurological pathways, they lead to financial abundance, if we can stay the course. In these early days, weeks, months, and years, we need to stay alert. It is common to slip back into what is comfortable, whether it serves us well, or not. Our minds and bodies do everything they can to stay in that comfortable state! Because our bodies and their mental patterns have developed to help us feel safe—we must show our inner child/inner parts of ourselves, that we *are* safe, and in control of this new freedom.

It's time we get comfortable being uncomfortable.

Our first experiences with money stem from an early age, in which we may have experienced trauma. Little "t", or big "T"—folks, trauma is trauma! Trauma becomes part of us, until we can work through it. Mindset is one thing; financial healing is another. We are not always aware of our own trauma. Our minds and bodies do a good job disassociating, to keep us safe. I kid you not, our behaviors and patterns stem from root wounds, within.

Many of us have experienced personal development and healing, however, we tend not to look at our finances as needing that same inner healing. That is what makes this financial wholeness journey so remarkable.

One thing I have found when bringing up the past, is that we are not trying to relive or reactivate the pain we endured. Some things throughout this book may be activating, as emotions stir, and things surface. Here is my encouragement for you: hold these beliefs in a neutral space. We need the space to feel it and release it. You will hear me often say, if we squash our emotions, they will show up in other ways. For me, it was undiagnosed health issues. A solid read on this topic is *The Body Keeps the Score: Brain, Mind, and Body in the Healing of Trauma* by Bessel van der Kolk.

Think of an emotion as an alarm going off, that is trying to tell us something. Now, if the fire alarm goes off in your house are you going to ignore it? (Presuming you are not cooking!) No, you would search the house for the cause! So, if our bodies are giving us an alarm, why do we so quickly push the off button? Trust me, I had mastered the off switch. Hell yeah, I was good at it! By doing that, my body remained in the sympathetic nervous system, the fight-or-flight response. We will touch on emotions in an upcoming chapter, not to worry. I will give you terrific tips and tricks to help self-regulate your emotions.

READER REFLECTIONS

It is now your turn to reflect on experiences that caught you by surprise, intrigued you, or have challenged you regarding money and emotions.

Chapter Three: Financial Wholeness

"I cheated on my fears, broke up with my doubts, got engaged to my faith and now... I am marrying my dreams."

–Unknown.

Wholeness is our goal. When we are whole, we live out a profound version of our most authentic selves. I love how Tiffany Aliche describes financial wholeness: "Financial wholeness is when all aspects of your life are working together for your greatest good, the biggest benefit, and richest life."

I break down the word "WHOLENESS," into an acronym:

W – Wisdom to walk in truth.

H – Holistic hope. (I never said this would be easy.)

O – Openness, curiosity, and possibility.

L – Let go, forgive, let the emotion move through you.

E – Eliminate unhealthy patterns, beliefs, and behaviors.

N – Navigate trusting yourself and others, through grace and compassion.

E – Explore and experience healthy boundaries with others.

S – Success is setting up healthy neurological pathways.

S – Seek support; no one gets there alone.

With this acronym you are equipped to do the work needed to reach financial wholeness.

W – Wisdom comes through mentorship. Do you honestly feel as though we have money mentors? If you do, that is terrific; you are ahead of the game. Having a mentor is someone who can help you to see your blind spots, someone who gives both positive and constructive feedback. Wisdom builds in many forms, whether people from different generations, books, podcasts, or interactions with others. Learning is everywhere! However, this is where I will caution you to use discernment when given knowledge. Does it align with the core of who you are? Are their morals and values like yours? If you have listened to my podcasts, you have heard me say, "Get the right damn people on your damn bus and the wrong ones off it."

Consider you are the average sum of the five people you spend the most time with. How are these people affecting your overall health and wellness, including your finances? Having the wisdom to know who is helping and who is hindering your financial future will help you to walk in your truth. Consider this your permission to tweak, pivot, overhaul, and fine-tune the wisdom you receive. Know the difference between niceness and kindness. I used to think they were interchangeable, and they are not. I'll take you down that rabbit trail a bit later.

H – Holistic hope, a key ingredient to living well. We need hope in all areas of our lives to achieve wholeness. Our mental, physical, emotional, spiritual, and financial health are intertwined. Hope is believing in something, some say faith. I am not projecting my belief system on you here, not to worry. Faith means believing in something better, bigger, and more fulfilling. Everyone is called to live an abundant, prosperous future, without limits. I was given a piece of wall-art in my darkest days, and it read: "Do not fear the path that you have been given; the path becomes clear as you take the steps." I had to have hope and believe that something better was around the corner. This gave me faith that I could take even just the smallest step forward.

O – Openness, I wish it were a "C," if I am honest, but I can work with it. When we remain open, we allow for curiosity, and curiosity is the antidote to judgment! If you are judging yourself for past money mistakes, shift your mindset and be curious about what lies beneath your choices. What were the emotions or feelings that drove your behavior? Is there a story related to your choices? The judgments, embarrassment, and guilt dissipate when your mind gets curious about what is possible. Remain open to what feels right for you as you gain traction in your finances.

L – Let it go, let it go...okay, I may have seen Frozen too many times; I am a mom. This is not the first time that you have heard "letting go", is fundamental. If you are reading this, you have probably read other self-improvement books and many of them talk about unforgiveness being a life sentence that you are serving, if you cannot let go. Forgiveness and letting go was a big one for me, as I am a grudge-holder, resentment queen, and a Bitterness Betty. To learn to let things go had me digging deep within. I needed the pain to move through my mind, body, and spirit before the weight lifted. Sometimes it helps to journal and ask yourself what it costs you *not* to let it go. Is the cost worth it? I take my clients through a worksheet that helps release resentment and bitterness. They create awareness for themselves as they journal and reflect on their role in their own situation. This phrase hit me like a freight train: "Life is not happening to you; it is responding to you." These words rattled me longer than I would like to admit. Radical responsibility helps us to let go of the past and move forward.

E – Eliminating unhealthy patterns, beliefs, and behaviors. If we do not do the work, our bodies will keep the score of our financial stress. If you are a parent, your children are learning from you as you are continually modelling how you wish for them to live out their financial future. My guess is YOU want to have financial freedom and retire! This awareness requires your attention to how you are currently living out your money story today and into the future. Remember, we have both conscious and unconscious patterns that show up in how we interact with money. If you do not do the work, nothing will change, and you will stay stuck.

N – North can be referred to as your true north—navigating the most authentic version of yourself. Wholeness comes when we clarify who we are and where we are heading. A place of self-acceptance, grace, and compassion for ourselves, is necessary. This does not happen overnight. We have heart-wrenching and devastating stories that are part of our life lens. I learned an important message: our experiences, our lives, and our stories do not define who we are. You are not your circumstance or your past. You have a choice and you determine your future. So, grab hold of your steering wheel as you embark on this adventure! Better yet, I'll join you! Finding our true north requires determining who we are, to the core. I will take you deeper, in later chapters, to help you discover what makes up your core and how to stay true to your spirit, in all aspects of your life. There is only one YOU! Be it, in all spheres.

E – Explore a new way, one with healthy boundaries for the self and others. If we do what we have always done, we will get what we have always gotten. This may be foreign to you, or you may feel uncomfortable if you are not used to boundaries with yourself and others. It will get easier. Remember your job is to care for yourself; you cannot pour from an empty cup. I bet you are wondering what boundaries you need when it comes to your money. Have no fear, my wonderful readers; I will bring you the goods.

S – Success is rebuilding our minds and our healthy neurological pathways. Think about a gravel road. (Sorry, city folk! I am a country girl, and this is the best way for me to describe the old patterns in our brains.) Think of your old habits and behaviors that hinder your financial future, as the rut on a gravel road. This gravel road is muddy, and the grooves are deep. It has not been graded for a long time, meaning it is tough to forge a new path, and you might end up stuck. Hence, we need to build healthy, new pathways, and forge a *new* way to drive on the gravel road. It will take significant effort, slower speeds, determination, and intense focus not to fall back into the old ruts. Success is when we rebuild healthy pathways that take us where we want to go, and BEYOND!

S – Support is crucial, and you need the right people. No one gets there alone! Have accountability partners or create a vision board. Who can you pull in as a resource? Play to your strengths, play to the people you trust around you or bring in a professional to help. Remember, if you have a health concern you see a doctor. When you have a tooth problem, you go to the dentist. For money advice, see a professional. I love this aspect of my work as a money coach *extraordinaire*. I use unconventional wisdom that leads to true transformation. You are getting a sneak peek into my material, through this book. I hope you find it insightful and empowering. Community is essential and choosing the *right* community can be tricky. I suggest trying different communities on, as if were shopping for a pair of jeans. When you find that gem that fits exactly right, you will thank me. Do not forget that not all communities are for you, and it is okay to outgrow, or quit a community, if it no longer serves you well.

PERSPECTIVE SHIFT EXERCISE

I challenge you to shift your perspective around wholeness and money. Look back through the lenses. Review each letter from the WHOLENESS acronym and ask yourself what you were told about wisdom, what you learned about wisdom, and what you have experienced. Did you formulate a belief regarding the word wisdom? Now do the same for the word "hope", and so forth, until you have digested the concept of *wholeness*.

You may find hidden difficulties when you break down the word "wholeness." They may surprise or challenge you. This can stem from the four lenses of what you were told, learned, and experienced.

READER REFLECTIONS

What beliefs or feelings show up as you think about wholeness?

What is significant about wisdom, hope, observations, letting go, eliminating, navigating, exploring, success, and seeking?

If you are having difficulties, can you articulate what is preventing you from experiencing or taking the steps?

Chapter Four: How and Why This Works

"This above all: to thy own self be true."

–Shakespeare

Financial wholeness is no instant coffee approach! This is a process of becoming secure in oneself and knowing your self-worth, evaluating how it came to be. Choosing healthy self-perceptions, having boundaries, and building your tribe of people and your communities. We are dismantling thoughts of comparison, enjoying the fun things, and rewiring our neurological pathways to be whole. This process that we have crafted allows us time to soak and percolate. Can you tell I'm a coffee lover?

This is a brave space to be real, honest, and without judgment. I am sharing my stories, hoping you do not feel isolated or alone. The antidote to judgment is curiosity, which may sound like something I have said before. Well, it is! When something is repeated, it is worth remembering, so lean in with curiosity and possibility in all aspects of your life.

Throughout this book: *Rethink Your Financial Health* you will encounter bite-sized learning with practical applications. These require self-reflection, accountability and sitting with the uncomfortable at times. Leave room for complexity and healing and allow for flexibility as you release this old story that is hindering your success. Experiencing an "aha" moment helps to solidify the learning. Breakthroughs and letting go are things you can anticipate on our journey.

Here is how my concept works: this book will walk you through twenty chapters, in which we show up brave, unfiltered, as we share our stories in ways that educate and enlighten. Soak it all in, percolate! So much of this healing journey is paying attention to where in our bodies we store our anxiety, stress, worry, and fear.

I am a storyteller. These stories are not easy to share, as I have spent time healing from shame, embarrassment, and other negative emotions locked within my body. It has taken me time to process my own experiences to bring them to you. At no point have I figured it all out! "Progress over perfection" is my new favourite saying, thank you Dee. Stepping out into the unknown can be scary, and I am here with you and will be your guide.

Earlier, I promised to take you on a rabbit trail regarding the differences between niceness and kindness. This is the perfect opportunity, as kindness is saying and doing that hard thing, to bring about change. I'm not looking to be nice in this book, I am being kind. Everyone likes nice! Relationships go well when we are nice, we get promoted when we are nice, we are accepted when we are nice, nice is good at looking good. Nice is agreeable, friendly, and accommodating.

Niceness can also be deceptive when it is dressed up. It can be self-serving and entitled. It can be fragile and give up when not reciprocated. Niceness can be fragile (remind them what 'it' is), and it can give up when not reciprocated. So, think about this: what are your motives when you are nice? There are benefits to being "NICE", instead of being truthful and bold. Niceness can be people-pleasing, rather than authentic. I used to be nice in hopes that others would like me. Would you forgive a person's character flaws if they are nice to you? Sad, but we indeed, do.

Kindness is genuine, real, honest, and authentic. It has a rigid center and a soft outer layer. It is someone that stays true to their values, no matter what. Kindness demonstrates the courage to boldly love others when they are prickly to love, regardless of the outcome. Kindness says the hard thing, without predicting the outcome. How hard is that my dear ones? Kindness is speaking the truth, at all costs.

Learning and unlearning are equally important, as we look at the lenses through which we experience life. We must embrace the unknown and trust that everything is unfolding, just as it should. I wish to explain how your own lenses may bring forward resistance, which I do not want to diminish or minimize. When resistance shows up, it is our body trying to tell us something. There may be a reason it is uncomfortable, and it could be that we have been told, learned, or experienced something during our lives that may cause resistance to certain topics. If at any point throughout this book you feel activated or triggered, set it down, take a few deep breaths and reflect on why. Having additional support such as a therapist, counselor, or psychologist is always recommended, as things may surface that require their expertise.

You may feel ashamed because, as a kid, you were told, "Shhh, we don't talk about money," or you learned that money caused fighting and arguments in your family. If you have experienced manipulation around money, you will be guarded just hearing me say the word "manipulation". This is the reason we need to press in. You may have things come up that have nothing to do with money but everything to do with how you view your self-worth, like physical or sexual abuse, neglect, or abandonment. That is the beauty of this book; its unconventional wisdom is paired with storytelling. We touch on the hot topics in this book to bring awareness to what is acceptable and what is unacceptable behavior regarding your past experiences with money.

PERMISSION TO FEEL EXERCISE

You know the feeling that money brings up for you; it is essential to know that it is okay to feel these feelings! Feelings are neither good nor bad; they are merely feelings. Feelings are there to tell us that something bigger is going on. It is your job to play detective and find what is under the surface; that is the knowing.

Now, what do you believe about money? Deep down, do you believe it to be true? What would your future self say to this belief of yours? If you could live out your truth in any way, what would it look like? Take some time to write this down. Envision your future, and, of course, what is possible for you to live out—that is the doing.

Head knowledge.

Heart understanding.

Doing is the ability to live differently.

READER REFLECTIONS

Make three columns: one being your feelings in the present moment, a second column for what you envision the future holding for you, and a third, for what you feel when you think about your future.

Chapter Five: Lenses in Which We Do Money

"You can be rich with money, but to be wealthy, you need all the things that money can't buy."

–Unknown.

If you get anything from this book, hopefully you will come to understand there are lenses through which we look, that do not always represent the truth of the situation.

A lens is a transparent structure. It is a piece of glass or plastic shaped to focus or spread light rays that pass through it, often to form an image. There are different types of lenses: the human eye, magnifying glasses, eyeglasses, camera lenses, telescopes, microscopes, projectors—you get the idea. Each lens changes what we see; some give us more detail while others make things foggy. The lenses of what we are told, learn, and experience give us different views; they change our perception of how we see and interpret life's events.

The lens we look through can change our view of the truth. We tend to respond the same with the other two lenses; what we learned, and what we experienced. What does this mean? Our brain is made up of eighty-five billion neurons; all these neurons relay information to each other through a complex electrochemical process. Making connections from the five senses affects how you think, learn, move, and behave.

Our personal narrative is filtered through four lenses. What we were told often refers to a planted seed; the origin is a lie or belief about something that others might have told us throughout the years, not to mention the things we tell ourselves! This contributes to how we view the world and live in all areas of our lives, including our finances.

Imagine being told you were lazy as a kid, that you would not become anything. This creates a sense of low self-worth and self-doubt. As you grow older, you may face challenges getting a job. Now, what is the first thought bound to surface in your subconscious mind? You guessed it: "You are lazy," from that old, planted seed! You now create a story of laziness and live it out in a justifying manner. This is not always true. There are times when we can defy the odds. I know from experience, that even when we fight the odds of what was spoken over us, we live in a state of, "I will show you; I will prove to you, that I will make something of myself." Although this might have served you and I well in the past, we need to be aware of what perceptions are driving the bus.

The second filter is what we learned. Whether that be teachings in school, at home, on social media, watching others, or using all our senses to formulate a story. Once we have a story, we then seek proof to validate our story is real. These stories we develop and create in our subconscious and conscious minds, and we will do anything to find the evidence around us to solidify our thoughts and feelings. This is where danger lies. These are all lenses, and they are not the truth. It is perception.

A personal example from my upbringing, I learned the woman is the one who takes care of the finances. I love my dad to pieces, and he would be lost financially without my mom's leadership in this capacity. To be honest, he may not be able to write a check! (That is dating me and my parents. Sorry, Mom and Dad, ha-ha!) So, from seeing that demonstrated in my own family's dynamic, I feel that being the woman, I am supposed to manage the finances. In your household it might have been the other way around—the male figure took care of money and having to do it yourself gives you anxiety or stresses you out, as it did your mother. Neither of these examples is right or wrong. What messages are you hearing from your childhood and what lens are you looking through when it comes to your money?

Let us talk about the lens of experience. We all know that from our experiences, we generate a story—an elaborate one. Sometimes there can be truth in it, and other times it is made up in our minds, we just believe it to be true. Our experiences can be both good and bad, and they solidify the story within. When we experience something, all our senses are engaged. From there, we solidify our belief system which becomes heart knowledge. We live out this knowledge as beliefs, personal truth, values, and our moral compass.

Keep in mind, not all thoughts perceived through these lenses align subconsciously with our core values. We have patterns and behaviors that can go hog wild because we have not taken the time to take inventory of what we believe about such things. Engage in self-awareness of what adversity you have needlessly taken on. My friend, you have the power to shift and change your thoughts. Absolutely nothing is set in stone!

In this case, we are talking about money and financial health. Wealth comes from within, and we need to get clear on the truth of who we are and what we are worth. We must take inventory as to what is hindering our success or leading us towards a particular financial future.

MONEY REFLECTION EXERCISE

Think about what money was like in your home as a child. What was your first experience with money? Was there a scarcity mindset or an abundance mindset? Did your parents live paycheck-to-paycheck? Did they have wonderful things, and were you fortunate to have whatever you wanted? Or did you fit in the middle somewhere?

Next, think about what you remember. Did your family talk about money? Was it civil, or was it like walking on eggshells when the money topic came up? Was there an equal power balance between both parents? Can you remember the feelings that money gave you? Are they positive or negative? Now, think about how you carried these memories with you, all these years, through your very own patterns and behaviors. Are you able to identify some memories about money?

Growing up, we had different seasons of both scarcity and abundance. I recall it being stressful in the home when finances were tight. It was complex to understand at such an early age, how we could go on trips one year and then the next, we could not. When I married Bart, he had grown up in a vastly different financial environment than I did. He had a minimalist lifestyle, and his parents were old school and male dominated. He grew up with two older siblings. One of his memories of money was in terms of extracurricular activities at the school. You see, Bart was extraordinarily talented and athletic. His parents, however, would not pay for the sport he wanted to pursue, so when we started having a family, he made it truly clear that no matter what, we would make sure our kids would experience and pursue the things they loved. This brought me to a season, after his passing, when I had tremendous guilt and stress about my finances, but I knew how important it was to him that the kids remain in hockey, ringette, and gymnastics. The pressure that I put on myself to afford it all was debilitating, at times.

Can you relate to something within your own family dynamics? Perhaps you grew up in a home where your parents favored a sibling, or you witnessed your parents being drained of time and resources for a child with addictions. These events in your life, big or small, play a role in how you parent and live out our finances. Your parents had difficulty putting food on the table, so you vowed never to put limits on groceries. Your parents did not pay for your secondary education and now that you have kids, you want to help them, as you know firsthand the struggle and grind you faced. We can use our experiences as leverage to succeed financially, or let these stories hinder us and enable others. At times, this is a paradox, because we can experience both.

INVENTORY EXCERCISE

Now that you have examples for each lens, try an inventory of your own life. You might reflect on what you've been told, learned, and experienced. How did this help formulate your beliefs over the years?

What were you told about money?

What did you learn about money?

What did you experience throughout your life that has affected how you live out your finances? Good or bad.

How do you feel about these discoveries? Are you able to bring up moments and reflect on how your upbringing plays into your patterns and behaviors with money?

Is it the truth?

What would your future self say to this belief of yours?

What do you want your future self to believe and live out?

And, of course, with the truth, what is possible for you now and in the future?

Remember to write it down!

Any "oh shit" moments, or "aha" moments?

Are you finding these filters/lenses helpful?

READER REFLECTIONS

I encourage you to share with your family, spouse, and even your kids, some of the stories you are uncovering. Take this time to demonstrate learning and unlearning. So often I sat at the dinner table, explaining to my kids that, "Oh crap, your mom got this wrong. Time to course-correct; bear with me as I navigate."

A remarkable thing happens when you do this. Our family bonded, we became open to unlearning and relearning, giving and receiving feedback as we grow as a tribe. I hope you try it for yourself, to experience what I am referring to!

Chapter Six: What Our Parents Didn't Teach Us About Money

"The hardest financial skill is getting the goalpost to stop moving."

–Morgan Housel.
(Read that one again 😊)

I am sure we can all look back and think to ourselves, "Heck, my parents didn't teach me that!" Now, being a parent, I realize how easily that happens.

My kids always say to me, "But Mom, I do not remember you teaching me that." I assumed they would learn by watching, which is not always great, as I am far from perfect. The other day, my sixteen-year-old asked how to get to the tennis courts; he has driven with me countless times. But now that he is a solo driver he has no idea— he did not pay that close attention. My daughter did the same thing when she had to go to the eye doctor, she was unsure what to do or how to do it, even though she has gone for the last ten years. I had to walk her through having her health card, checking in at the desk, waiting her turn, and then paying when she was finished. We often throw out the phrase "common sense". I did that repeatedly, until one day, a gentleman retorted, "sometimes common sense isn't so common." I then had to ask what he meant, and he proceeded to explain that just because it makes sense to *me* does not mean it will make sense to *everyone*. At that moment, I felt slapped in the face as I recalled a memory from a corporate environment, where there was an expectation of me, and I had no idea! I told my senior manager, "If you had that expectation do you not think it would have been a clever idea to inform me? By not informing me, you are setting me up for failure." He responded with, "common sense." I guess I missed that memo, of what was common sense and what was not. It happens. Instead of assuming that others know, we need to be more thorough, clear, concise, and informative. That is why I bring you this chapter: things I wish I knew sooner—sharing the manual my friends.

I know there is not enough education or discussion about the psychology of money. Our choices, patterns, and behaviors, all have a trend. We talk numbers, and bring up terms such as TFSA, RRSP, RESP, and so forth, but the foundation of money is really in our minds and emotions. A quote from Ayn Rand is quite relevant here: "Money is only a tool. It will take you wherever you wish. But it will not replace you as the driver." I had to read that a couple times for it to really sink in.

If you are not a good driver, you are in trouble. It takes practice and time to become a good driver; this does not happen overnight. The same is true for managing money—it takes practice, trial, and error. We might get it wrong, but what if we can eliminate the significant screw-ups for others, regarding money? Wouldn't that be amazing? I tell my kids, all the time, to learn from my mistakes. They often chuckle and bring up, "But Mom, failure is where the best lessons are!" (My kids are a bunch of wise asses, just saying.) So many of us were not given the basic elements when it came to our money. Often, we learned through trial and error. There is a better way—the information highway. Education and awareness give *you* the power to make more informed choices, which is beautiful.

I have this book, and as I am skimming the chapter titles, I have to say, they are remarkable. To name a few: "Man in the car paradox—no one is impressed with your possessions as much as you are." "Are we that vain?" It is as if we are brainwashed to believe such nonsense.

This holds weight, and it could be the words that are spoken to us directly, or words we have overheard people say. These things, planted within us at such an early age, may not be the truth but we live so much of our lives believing they are. Here is a prime example: I spent some time with a young couple who are missionaries, and they mentioned something that I found interesting: "Others expect us to be poor." I had to think about that for a second, if we were to unpack what they believed, it would stem from what others, within their communities or organizations, have told them. It is a limiting belief that is not true at all! I know missionaries that do abundantly well and take that opportunity to generate more opportunities for others. I have another fitting example, and this one is true of how

I grew up. If you mentioned the word "insurance" around my parents, they had their opinions. I was already bitter without knowing the cost of car insurance; and believed home insurance was a fraud until I needed to make a claim, and life insurance. Well, for those of you who know my journey of being widowed without a plan, this is one that I will never take for granted again, based on what I now know to be true. At the time, though, my views on insurance were filtered through what I was told: "Those sketchy insurance salesmen/women cannot be trusted." This was my lens.

We learn things from all aspects of our world, people, places, music, television, schools, social media, and the list goes on. Our minds take in so much information and store it. When things are repeated, reiterated, or in front of us all the time, they start to take up space in our subconscious minds. Let us take Christmas, for example, when the television commercials are blasting—advertising the latest and best toys. Or, back in the day, the Sears catalogue that we used to create our Santa list. I quickly learned that I wanted a Cabbage Patch doll, but had I not seen it or heard about it, I would not have known any different. So, guess what my parents did? They got me that Cabbage Patch doll. The programming worked. How does this concept now apply to our money? The same is true; let us look at a big bank's commercials playing non-stop during COVID, talking about how they could offer us money using a home equity loan, or line-of-credit, to do home renovations. Was it in the best interest of homeowners to do that? Not always—yet people did.

Another splendid example is Wayfair's commercial, where two families are competing with one another. First, the neighbor gets a touch-tap sink and then the other installs a stereo in the shower. The commercial finishes with a mailbox shot saying, "Jones." Think about this for a second: this teaches us to compete with others, to gain an advantage over our neighbor. They were making us feel lack, or fear missing out. Let's be honest; I have fallen for it. My friends just got a new vehicle, and suddenly I want one too! No one is immune to this, but what we are *not* taught, is to look out for the signs, or to recognize the emotions that are telling us a bigger problem is at bay.

We are going to talk about emotions around money in the upcoming chapters. So many financial decisions are driven by feelings, whether we recognize them, or not.

This is what my parents did not teach me about money: the power of our minds, the conscious and subconscious beliefs we have stored up throughout our lives, and the lenses we move through life with.

Let us look at the lens of our experiences, or those to which we were close. How did they impact how we live out our money? What did our parents teach, or not teach us? When you were a young kid and your mom was cooking in the kitchen, how often did she tell you not to touch the stove? Now, if you are like me and like to learn the hard way, you went to touch the stove and burned your hand. That is the best lesson—instantly it cauterized in your mind (did you like that?), that the stove is hot, and when you touch it, pain comes. In life, not all lessons are that fast or instilled that quickly. But our minds can store up a lifetime of good and bad experiences, and these correlate with our feelings, emotions, and responses.

Are you wondering how your own experiences have played a part in your finances? I hope you are pondering that great question. I like examples to drive this home: a young man grew up in a family that did well, and he was given everything he needed. His parents gave him a credit card and covered the bill. (You may be thinking to yourself that it must be nice, right? But wait, this is a hard lesson; I am not sure if I would want it.) So, he grows up and gets his *own* credit card and charges things without putting any thought into how to pay it off—remember that was not his experience— and is now facing an astronomical amount of credit card debt. Unable to manage his affairs, he declares bankruptcy. This affects the next ten years or more, hindering his future.

Now, let me share my experiences with money, from a different angle. I used money as a form of numbing the emotional pain I was feeling—always looking for the next feel-good moment, a car, a trip, vacations, adventures, clothes, jewelry—you name it, I numbed myself with it. I tried to fast-track our grieving journey with money, and I did not even know I was doing it. I did not understand that money and emotions even went together.

If you took a moment to self-reflect on the psychological side of money, where do your emotions come into play? You will likely be shocked with what you uncover. I wish I had learned about the psychological side of money earlier in life. Instead I now get to bring awareness to others about the power emotions can have over your money.

That is, until you shed light on these emotions. At this point you can harness control and make better financial decisions.

The last filter, is what we believe to be accurate, based on what we were told, learned, and experienced. When we think something is true, our actions reflect that. I often use the "Know, Believe, Do" model, and tell clients it is their life raft to use, especially in terms of money. I say that because we frequently have a blockage—I know I do. I know in my head what I need to do, but I don't do it! Can anyone else relate? This happens more times than I would like to admit—it's a good thing for grace. So, how do we get head knowledge to heart knowledge? Well, that is a loaded question, and I am not sure I know the answer quite yet. It takes consistency, persistence and intention to cancel out the lie that is blocking the truth from really hitting home. This is a great place to start.

When we know in our hearts the truth about money, we can pull the weeds, which are the lies that creep in from the world. You know the ones: instant gratification, competition, feeling you have earned it, you're not enough, you need more, just hustle charge it and pay later. There's also that scarcity mindset, hoarding money, and so on.

I want to hit on more things our parents did not teach us about money: shame, embarrassment, superiority complexes, money infidelity/secrecy, and money obsession. These are destructive behaviors and generational money traumas that are passed down— they boil down to financial abuse. I hope you are listening and realizing that there is much more to money than just numbers. And when these issues arise or exist within family dynamics, achieving financial wholeness is hard. The ability to reach your finish lines can be hijacked by one, or more, of these issues. Without recognizing this or bringing awareness to it, we cannot make the necessary changes needed to reach fulfillment.

This one, I know, makes people laugh. It is the story I usually tell when I mention money infidelity: my good old Amazon package that comes in the mail, that I hide. Let us call a spade, a spade—I do it. I have even been on the devastating side of this one. Partners that had credit cards in secret or were stashing money and incurring debt without any discussion or agreement. This is secrecy at its finest! I know I am not the only one who has been on both sides of this coin but let us be honest, who is willing to own it and take radical responsibility for what may be underneath these patterns? How are we educating ourselves and our children about traps that are out there when making wise decisions?

Let me ask you a question - if you had talked about money in this way within your family dynamics or relationships, would it have changed your financial future?

Here are the common money disorders that you need to be aware of:

- Compulsive spending: we know this one.

- Hoarding money: yes, people hoard cash.

- Workaholism: real in my home, always striving for more, getting to the next level. "If only I had this, I would be happy."

- Gambling: is it hidden; would you recognize the signs?

- Financial enabling as parents: we can do this with the best intentions. This was me as a mom—it was more about me and my unresolved emotions of guilt, and shame that had me enabling my kids. I was making financial decisions for them, paying for everything, and feeling taken advantage of. I couldn't say "no", then I would harbor resentment. Unable to hold true to my boundaries, I was continually caving. I felt as though I owed them; they didn't ask to be fatherless. I didn't want them to struggle. But it is time we become aware of what is healthy and what is not. Are we setting our kids up or are we hindering their financial future in hopes to tame our own guilt, blame, or shame? Managing our own money teaches us grit and perseverance. If we always bail them out, they don't learn coping tools or strategies.

- Money enmeshment: I will be honest; I had to look this one up. Money enmeshment is when we share inappropriate financial information with our children. We might include them in ugly financial affairs, argue about money with kids in earshot, or use a child or teen to manage debt collectors. Couples in a custody battle inappropriately informing the kids as to what is happening. When we overshare information that is not age-appropriate or even relevant to children or teens, it has lasting effects on them. When they get older, they will have to work through this trauma they endured.

I must be careful here, looking back, as I recognize an area that was gray for me. After Bart passed away, I was a single mom raising my three kids. "We are a single-family household, no, you cannot have new hockey gloves because we do not have two incomes like those other families!" I have had to come to terms with the fact that it was wrong of me to say those things to my kids. It was unhealthy and gave them a false view of families with two incomes or even the diligent single-income homes that could afford it. My tone and choice of words gave them a sense of scarcity, embarrassment, and jealousy. They wanted what others had and were not content with what I was providing. *I* imposed that; *we* must work at dismantling this, as a family.

PASS THE BATON EXERCISE

It is crazy to think how our words and actions can make such lasting impacts. A money mindset is what you believe about money, yourself, the world, and how your life unfolds. Every day, you have the power to choose what will move you forward or backward.

Now, if you are ready to be brave, I am prepared to take you to financial wholeness. When we unlearn and relearn things our parents taught us about money, we demonstrate to the next generation what true financial freedom is. Take your family along for the ride and share what you are learning from this book: Rethink Your Financial Health.

READER REFLECTIONS

Try writing out all your beliefs about money and ask yourself where they came from.

Is my belief about money true?

What is under that belief?

Was I told that?

Did I learn it?

Have I experienced it?

What is the truth about your money belief?

When you look back at what your parents did not teach you about money, or even what you have not prepared for your own kids, can you recognize the importance of viewing money differently? Put thought into how you are living out your words, actions, and experiences and what you might be demonstrating to others watching. Do you need to shift and change in some areas?

Chapter Seven: Insecurities & Limiting Beliefs

"If you believe you can or can't, either way, you are right."

–Unknown

You have heard lots of buzz about "limiting beliefs". You may even be working through your own with a counselor, coach, friend, or family. That is why this quote is so fitting: causes of our limiting beliefs develop at an early age.

Remember my references to the four lenses? What we were told, learned, and experienced, all contributes to formulating our belief system.

The "what we are told" lens, refers to words that have been spoken over us, words we have overheard, or things we hear.

The "what we learned" lens could be things we have seen demonstrated, teachings at school, things our parents taught us, conversations we overheard, lessons we learned from television, social media, the world around us.

The lens of experience includes all our senses and what happened to us or others close to us.

These lenses are relevant. Often, limiting beliefs stem from a negative experience that has left an impression. Here is an excellent example of my own limiting belief, that I created and manifested in my life: the "black sheep." I may have been a challenging teenager; I did things the hard way and gave my parents a run for their money. My brother was the "golden child." I still, to this day, use these terms. It does not mean they are true. I formulated this belief system from things I saw, heard, and learned. Then, my feelings hijacked all rationale and created this negative story in my head: that I was not good enough, that I was the odd one out, that I would not make anything of myself. My list can go on and on.

Here are some examples of other limiting beliefs:

I am not good enough.

I am not smart enough.

I will fail.

Terrible things always happen to me.

I am not going to find Mr. Right or Mrs. Right

Rich people are greedy.

I am invisible.

I cannot do anything right.

Money is the root of all evil.

I am not qualified for that job.

I am too old.

I will be happy when _____ happens.

I need love and approval from others.

To be worthwhile or worthy, I must achieve and succeed.

Can you hear yourself in these sentences? I know I can. I always ask my kids, "Do you speak to your friends the way you speak to yourself?" I hope the answer is always "no." We should ask ourselves instead, "Why do I not deserve the same kindness, love, and compassion, I give to others?" It often comes down to our own self-worth. We are going deep, my friends—who else struggles with their self-worth? If left unchecked, our limiting beliefs can sabotage our future (I say 'our' as I am not immune to this stuff). We are in this together. Limiting beliefs keep us stuck and unable to tap into our full potential. The sad truth is that we immediately assume we cannot do something before we even consider doing it!

I was challenged by this after Bart died. I was paralyzed with fear, and I did not know how to do things on my own. I grew up in a home where my dad always drove. My mom was the navigation system. She had her old, paper road map, with the highlighted route. My belief system from that experience was that you needed two people to travel, and my adventures came to a screeching halt as a single mom. I knew I wanted more and better for my kids; I did not want them to believe that they could not do anything in life, so I pulled on my big girl panties, and we drove to Ontario to visit family. Through the US, we went to the next stop, Chicago. We hit every Great Lake that trip, so we could dip our toes in the water and tell tales. It was remarkable, but it did not go off without a hitch, let me tell you. My GPS took me underground in Chicago; sure enough, I had four men approach my car: "Listen, Ma'am, this is how this will go… you will pay us, and we will give you directions on how to get out of the underground." I damn near shit my pants. Honestly, I do not know how much money I gave them or if I even heard the directions. I was praying fast and thinking we were all going to die. Then the voices got louder, telling me that I was stupid and crazy to think I could do this alone, without a man. Clearly it ended okay, as I am here authoring this book. Was the fear real? Hell, yes! Did I push through it? YES, but I had to change my limiting belief into an empowering thought: "I will take it slow and navigate this big city the best I can. I am a strong, independent woman. I will use both Google Maps and the vehicle navigation system. We got this." My kids looked at me and repeated my old mantra, "Mom, you ducking got this."

Here is a funny story about my "ducking got this". Everyone repeatedly asked if I was okay after Bart died. I would then retort, "YES, I fucking got this." My kids did not hear me swear often. It was not my style, but I was so damn tired of being interrogated. Then one day, my kids said, "Mom, swearing does not look good on you. Let's change it to 'ducking.'" Sweet, I ducking got this, quack-quack, baby! This mantra got me through one of my most challenging seasons, and I even got a duck tattoo to remind myself. I know, right? Who does that? When others see the duck on my foot, it makes for a great icebreaker.

Here are examples of what challenging limiting beliefs can look like:

- **Limiting Belief:** "I am too old to change careers."

    ○ **Empowering Belief:** "My age means that I bring life experience and wisdom to the table."

- **Limiting Belief:** "I will never be successful unless I have a degree."

    ○ **Empowering Belief:** "My success is determined by how hard I work, not my education level." This one gets me to my core; I dropped out in grade ten, got a full-time job and did things the hard way. I did end up going back and finishing. But my entire life, I have been judged, and I considered myself less than others for not doing it the same way as everyone else. Through my experience, I have learned there are multiple ways to get where you are going. It is about the journey, not the destination.

- **Limiting Belief:** "What will others think?"

    ○ **Empowering Belief:** "What people think of me and what I am doing is their problem. I am doing what is suitable for me."

We spend so much of our lives living for others; we need to take back control.

I love the phrase by Glennon Doyle: "It is your job to disappoint as many people as possible as long as you do not disappoint yourself." Think about how we can put limiting beliefs on our kids. This is not intentional at all, but through our words and actions, we display behaviors to those watching us. Kids especially pick it up subconsciously. They, too, have lenses and are looking for anything to validate the beliefs they have conjured up, from what they were told, learned, and experienced.

Let us talk about common money-limiting beliefs:

- I will never be able to retire.

- I cannot take time off. I have bills to pay.

- I am not worthy of that promotion or a newly available job.

The last one is real for many of us. *You have been offered a promotion at your job.* You know you can do the job. It is a pay increase which would be amazing; you could get out of debt faster and save for that new car that you wanted. Then it hits you—George in the office is a better fit. Or, if you are making more money, things will change, and your friend group may get jealous. You begin to think back about things you were told as a kid: you only need 'enough', money is the root of all evil, money changes people, men get promotions, not women can you see the stuck pattern? You can go around in a hamster-wheel with these old lies, your whole life! Changing these patterns is arduous work. It is no easy task.

THE FIVE R'S EXCERCISE

How do we recognize our limiting beliefs?

That is a great question, which often begins with "I can't, I am not, I don't have, I'll never, etc." Journaling is a wonderful way to formulate your thoughts and find the root of the limiting beliefs you still have and that are rearing their ugly heads.

Tip on working through limiting beliefs:

- **Recognize it:** Call it out, whatever it is—what are you feeling and where in the body do you feel it?

- **Reflect:** Where is this feeling coming from; what is the underlying reason it surfaced?

- **Rebuke it/Refuse it:** It is not the truth. It is a lie; reject the thought.

- **Reframe it:** Write out an empowering belief that cancels out the lie. Stay curious and ask yourself, what if I am wrong? What is possible, how is this belief serving me, and what could be different?

- **Reposition yourself:** Speak out the empowering belief repeatedly—there is power in mantras. Live out differently by doing one thing that brings you closer to the future you.

Why do you think the high-five habit goes viral? Must love Mel Robbins. Great ways to rewire your neurological pathways, Gabby Bernstein books/YouTube shorts, and *Immunity to Change,* by Kegan and Lahey. So many books that will help you to show self-love and to demolish the old limiting beliefs. But first, you must be a detective and find them, journal about them, and look back to where they have hijacked your greatness.

Take back your control now that you know. Give yourself grace for not being aware of it. I've read a book called *No Bad Parts,* by Richard Schwartz. It is incredible to think of how complex we are! We have many parts, and they each have a role to play. Their current role may not be the original design, but these parts have had to show up in diverse ways to keep us safe, protect us, shelter us, care for us, and so forth. The work Schwartz talks about is getting curious as to why your parts have had to operate the way they do and whether it is serving or hindering you. Great read.

What I have found helpful is working through my limiting beliefs with emotional tapping, positive affirmations, prayer, meditation, and mapping it out/journaling. Much of my work stems from being caught in a storm. I use that experience to teach you how to get through your own storms. A financial crisis is significant for us. I have been hit a couple of times by this storm. There is a way out, and this book can be your manual for working through the hard things we face, regarding money and life.

What do you think of when you hear about limiting beliefs? I refer to a state of mind or opinion about myself, that hinders me somehow. These beliefs are often false accusations we make about ourselves and bring about a negative result. The worst part is that we seek to validate our false, limiting beliefs, in the outside world. We do this subconsciously, when we seek to find things in our lives that confirm and solidify what we believe to be true. We want to validate the lie. We earnestly look for proof and can even create stories to back it up.

I lived my life being the misfit—I never fit in. Fast forward into my mid-thirties; I was moving into a corporate setting. Here I was, a little farm girl, mixing in with city folks with fancy letters after their names. I would often hear, "You're not corporate enough," and "What letters do you have after your name?" These comments stung me. My retort was always, "Hell, I am street-smart. I've got some real-life experience." I said it confidently. A friend of mine has a saying, "confident bullshit"—it's great. But inside I was hurting and feeling as if I was a fraud, not qualified, the underdog. Imposter syndrome took over my life! Not smart enough, not good enough, and my list goes on.

Let us bring back the lenses we keep talking about. This example is based on things I was told, but I took it even further. I began to say them to myself and guess what started to show up in my life? Evidence that validated this belief/lie about myself. Whenever something went wrong, I'd think, "I'll never be successful," or, "I don't have enough experience." So, now here I am, wallowing in my self-pity, manifesting *more* of what I *don't* want. Not only was I told that I was not smart enough, but I also learned it because I could not understand material as fast as others or got questions wrong on an exam. I would beat myself up over it, trying to be a perfectionist. To top it all off, experiences of failure solidified my belief that I must be a loser who is not smart enough. Please tell me I am not alone in these feelings! I hope you are chuckling and can relate too.

Then, I had a sweet soul tell me that life was not happening *to* me. It was *responding* to me! It makes for a great slap in the face when you reflect on that. I was creating what I feared the most. What you fear, you create. Take that catchy phrase with you, and the next time you are in fear, think of a way to change it to an empowering statement.

Another common, limiting belief is fear of failure—this one is big for me (crap, now that I have read over all of these, I seem to have faced them all, lol), and others in my family. I was out for coffee with a gentleman and I asked him, "What do you think stops a lot of people?" He replied, "Fear of success." I was taken aback, thinking, why would anyone fear success? That sounded stupid. Sure enough, I was digesting his comment for the entire two-hour drive home. Could it be true that we fear success so much that we sabotage our future? I began researching, to get other takes on it. Limiting beliefs are stories we tell ourselves, about who and what we are, that hold us back from becoming who we are truly meant to be.

We always circle back to our lenses; that is where the root of the belief is. There is always a story to uncover and unpack, to break apart the lie, and live out our best life. Remember, financial wholeness is a profound way of healing and living in alignment: when all aspects of your life are working together for your greatest good, the biggest benefit, and your richest life.

Ask yourself what limiting beliefs you were told. Is there something that you learned through your interactions with others? What have you experienced about the limiting belief, which has helped to solidify who you are? Can you recognize your limiting beliefs or are they still in disguise? This happens and it is okay. It could be a form of self-protection—your inner child may not be ready to work through the story behind the belief yet. I had this for a long time, regarding Bart's passing. Our traumatic events have a way of really overhauling who we are and how we show up.

We have protector parts within us. In knowing and understanding internal family systems, therapy allows us to differentiate between who we are and what we have done. We can have more compassion, as we understand our inner working parts and how they serve us by protecting us. I will briefly describe this and recommend you read more about IFS: *Internal Family Systems,* by Richard C. Schwartz.

Managers take on a pre-emptive, protective role. They protect us from harm and prevent our painful, traumatic experiences from flooding our conscious minds. Here are a few examples of our internal managers and how they can show up.

- People Pleaser

- Perfectionist

- Controller

- Busybody

- Inner Critic

- Multi-Tasker

Exiles isolate from other parts of our system. They represent our wounds, traumas, and the pain and fear we carry.

- Overwhelm

- Anxiety

- Depression

- Isolation

- Fear

- Shame

Firefighters work hard to deflect attention away from our hurt, leading to impulsive and unhealthy behaviors.

- Avoider

- Blame Shifter

- Acting Out/Rage

- Dissociation

- Self-Harm

- Numbing with alcohol, drugs, social media, sex, dating, etc.

Aligned Centered—The True You.

- Core Values

- Calm and Creative

- Confident

- Connected

- Compassionate

- Curious and Courageous

This work is unique because it is time that the true you, inside, comes to the surface. You are gifted beyond measure. I get excited, knowing you are working through these exercises, as I know what they were able to do for me. I pray that these exercises help reshape your entire life, to one of love, joy, peace, and abundance.

This work is important because our heads, hearts, and our actions, all work simultaneously. So often we know the truth in our minds but are unable to change our behaviors because there is a roadblock in the way!

Our insecurities come into play; there is a link between money, self-esteem, and our financial future. We have been socially conditioned to believe that our work makes us valuable, depending on our role. This creates a link between occupation, identity, and money. To no surprise, we view our self-worth based on our financial standing.

Our self-worth is abstract; it can not be measured. Money can—debt totals, bank balances, annual incomes, and our net worth. When our self-worth is based around money, our value can change in a moment; it shifts like shadows. Too many uncontrollable variables are a rollercoaster of emotions when we link the two. This takes a toll on our mental health, which plays a role in our physical health, over a more extended period.

We can tie our self-worth to many things, not just our money or job title. The list is long: our physical appearance and our academic success, who our partner is, who our parents are, where we live, and what we drive. It has also been said that people with low self-esteem and a lack of self-love have roots of unhealthy spending habits and patterns, as they seek material things. Materialism promises satisfaction but yields hollow remorse. Society exploits insecurities and generates more of them, through this cycle.

Breaking this link is challenging! A fitting example is if we have zero net worth, we may feel zero self-esteem; we then think back and find proof to solidify our belief system about ourselves: "I am nothing; I have nothing." These ingrained belief systems were planted long ago but let's be honest—we water them and what we water, will grow. You feed a teenage kid; sure enough, they grow and so does your grocery bill. Watering your lifestyle will only increase the cost of your lifestyle.

Our thoughts about our self-worth have become unruly and unmanageable, wreaking havoc on our relationships with others and the ones with ourselves—keeping us stuck. The insecurity cycle continues and grows; a recipe for disaster as more ingredients get added. Not good-looking enough, not smart enough, not sexual enough, not physically fit enough—do you see the "not enough" mindset showing up, over and over? When we are insecure, we are either in proving mode, striving, and pleasing people, or the other side, which is victimhood, wallowing, isolation, and dissociation. We want to have self-compassion, self-acceptance, self-love, as we are worthy of a different future.

How you feel about yourself does impact your bottom line. Make sure to distinguish the order. First, your self-worth is what you believe to be true about yourself and your future. So, if you have a poor opinion about yourself, you won't feel worthy. Then, you won't ask for that raise, and inconvertibly, you will experience lack, causing you to lack confidence in yourself. Do you see the correlation?

The life you wanted/had will wither away, just as your self-worth has. Unlinking your net worth from your self-worth means redefining who you are and your identity. Who are you as a person, outside of work? What are your core attributes? Take an inventory of the important character traits you demonstrate that have nothing to do with money or the world around you. Your self-worth should be based on your personal attributes. This is where you are aligned with yourself, *your character is enduring,* and it won't change when your bank account changes, your job changes, your relationship status changes, or your health changes. The goal is to have stable self-worth as your foundation. From there, you build, and naturally a sound net worth grows, not the other way around!

I will be very real and honest about how this has played a role in my life for many years. I had many seasons where my identity was tied to things. I'll take you down memory lane. I was the best mom ever, when my kids were younger. Homemade baby food, story time, crafts, and field trips. I was a wife that could do it all: cook, clean, care for the kids, stay fit, hunt, hang with the boys, and manage the bookkeeping for the business. Check, check, and check. But then, it all fell apart—my world *and* my identity, which was tied to the things of this world. I had misplaced who I was, which took me on a self-discovery journey. I needed to find myself, after Bart passed away. I was no longer the excellent wife and great mom.

Some time passed and I could tell "She's back!" I figured out who I was, to my core. I was secure in my identity. In a season of authentic alignment, I knew who I was— fearfully and wonderfully made to impact this world, and to serve others. I was operating in my core energy of femininity, which resulted in love finding its way to me. (We will touch on this in chapter fifteen.) I remarried, keep in mind I had been on this road before, of being engaged but not being able to quite pull the trigger and follow through with it. My kids laughed and thought I would be a runaway bride; I even wore running shoes underneath my dress— but this time, I did it.

Then, in year one of our marriage, I got hit with some health challenges that rocked my world. So, here I was, losing movement in my right leg, the functionality of my hands became questionable as they gave out randomly, and this was paired with my inability to have others touch me without feeling like my body was crawling with fire ants. I was bouncing between the sympathetic and dorsal nervous systems—I went from feminine energy to masculine fast, and my identity was again, compromised. A health curveball I never anticipated came my way. I was a runner, hiker, biker, tennis player, and an active mom. Not one that sat on the sidelines.

Here I thought I had figured out who I was. That is until I could no longer be their mom who played tennis, biked with my son or ran with my daughter without fear of her having to carry me home. Or being unable to please my husband whose love language is touch. I had to count on my kids moving me to bed more times than I would care to admit. I was unable to walk and being stuck in bed with pain had me questioning who I was or if I was even enough for those around me. So, I masked up to those closest to me.

When our insecurities come out to play, we come out of alignment with our core energies (feminine or masculine). This sends us between the fight, flight, freeze, or fawn central nervous system responses and sometimes even dissociation. At the time, I didn't see what this was doing to me, my kids, or my marriage. I was caught up in micromanaging everything and preparing for the worst. Sure enough, it happened: exactly what I feared. I created a husband who couldn't see, know, or understand me, anymore. I drove a wedge between us that only played on his insecurities and mine—leaving us both with unregulated emotional distress. Our decision making skills are far from optimal when operating with a dysregulated nervous system. Facing broken trust, shattered foundations, and our toxic unhealthy relationships with sex and money left us hopeless and in despair.

I share this, as it is essential to remember that our core energies, self-worth, emotional regulation, trauma, and insecurities play out in all realms of our lives, even hijacking our financial futures.

Here is a thought: instead of focusing on changing what we base our self-worth on, our focus should be on connecting our attributes and activities to goals beyond ourselves—connecting to others, serving, helping, and giving. This allows us to contribute to society. No easy task, mind you—getting aligned with self and a bigger purpose is where true happiness is found.

First, we need to stop with negative self-talk and comparing ourselves to others. When we align ourselves with purpose, regardless of how much we will earn, we value and appreciate our decisions, life choices, and personal achievements. When we can do this, our self-esteem is not swayed by money or the lives of others. It is a choice that impacts our emotional, physical, and mental health.

Through this, I have chosen to learn more about my body. Through trauma, emotional regulation, the art of holding space, polyvagal theory, feminine and masculine energy, and internal family systems, I have learned how to help my body heal. We must start listening and recognizing when our bodies give us alarm bells, indicating something isn't right and that we are offline.

I am grateful for the vast knowledge that I have gained about myself through my health and marital challenges, as our struggles are our most prominent teachers.

You've likely heard me say "Be it until you become it!" With this I am not referring to being fake...need. What I mean is, you may be playing off the attributes already within you and are living them out to a greater purpose. Ask yourself what ignites you and what core attributes bring pleasure. For me, it is being creative. I love creating things, whether a social media post, marketing material, writing, quilting, or scrapbooking. For many years I squashed this, and I have examined what is deep within me that needs to be expressed. Creativity, storytelling, and serving others through my healing journey, fuels my purpose. You see, it's bigger than me. I wake up every morning and ask myself how I will serve the world today; I trust my inner knowing, so I stay aligned.

Here are a few more examples: I want to be an author, so I must put pen to paper and write. My tagline is "Sharing the Manual", so I show up and authentically share the journey that has brought me here. I want to be viewed as fun, light-hearted, and joyful, so I have had to change my life to implement more fun, rest, and feminine energy. It's not pretending, I have had to implement change. That change will bring me closer to the results I want. You, too, will have to do the same.

The first place to start is to align yourself with the core of who you are: your character, attributes, and values. We talked about my core having a creative element but it also holds integrity, honesty, transparency, and is heart-centred. No matter what happens, I remain those things, regardless of my bank account, relationships, or health status.

Then ask yourself what *you* long for, dream of, and envision for *your* future. Finally, be sure to silence others, and yourself (the inner critic). Give space for the true you to speak up and show you who you really are and what your made of.

Confidence, self-worth, and insecurities come down to having a root cause. Your job is to be the detective and discover why, when, and where this belief about yourself was planted. If you don't do the inner work, your finances will stay the same for the long haul. You will hit the ceiling and revert to what is comfortable if you are unwilling to be uncomfortable. Being uncomfortable allows for healing, growth, and change to be implemented and wholeness achieved. When we heal, we engage with lost parts of ourselves—not looking to change or better them. Instead, we get to *accept* them.

Any movement toward wholeness must begin with acknowledgment of our suffering and our experiences. We must open ourselves to the truth of our lives, past and present—objectively and more matter-of-fact: this happened. We recognize where we were wounded and can honestly reflect on the impact this had on us and others—a radical responsibility for one's life.

I talk about the "Know, Believe, Do" model. "Know" being your head knowledge, "Believe" being heart understanding, and "Do" being the ability to live out differently, as the head and heart work simultaneously. It's been said by Gabor Mate explains that our hearts are our best compass on the healing path; the mind— conscious and unconscious—is the territory being navigated. Healing brings the two in alignment and cooperation.

This, my friends, is a moment-by-moment commitment that takes patience, curiosity, and grit. We are reconsidering and reconstructing our entire view. Mario Martinez says: "Healing cannot occur if we do not accept our worthiness—that we are worth healing, even if doing so might shake up our view of the world and how we interact with others."

When we believe something to our core, it is easy to move forward or complete a task. However, if there is any hesitation then we can, and often *do,* get hijacked. Then, we stay stuck. There is no easy fix to believing something different than what you have carried for years—which was the lie. I have mantras, reminders, visuals, tattoos, and songs that help me remember the truth about my value, my purpose, and my future. You get to creatively find what works best for you. An enemy is trying to steal, kill, and destroy your best self. I am here to let you know that you are valued, worthy, capable, and will kick ass at this work and reach financial wholeness because YOU want it badly enough!

FUTURE SELF EXCERCISE

Please, close your eyes and think about what *your* ideal future looks like. What does it smell like? What are you wearing? Who is around you? What is the environment like? What is the mood? Where in your body do you feel it? What are the sensations? I love this exercise. I will even step forward when I close my eyes, as if I am stepping into a new and improved version of myself. This exercise is excellent as it shifts your mindset and cancels your limiting beliefs. This somatic practice connects the mind, body, and spirit using physical and psychotherapy technique. Judgment cannot live where there is curiosity. When we imagine our future selves, we stay curious about what the future holds; we are open to receive. Do this exercise often: if you are feeling stuck, step back and then step forward and say aloud, "I am stepping into the best version of my future self."

If this is hard for you the first, second, or even third time, that is okay. Continue to do it! You will have breakthroughs; resistance is natural. I would imagine myself laughing, on a stage sharing stories, connecting with others on a very intimate level, kicked back in a chair with my legs dangling over the edge, wearing my favorite leopard vans, with a punch of pink on my lips. It was comfortable, calm, and energizing. Now it's your turn to imagine your future self. Write down what you experienced, even if it was nothing, or you felt it was stupid. Something may surprise you, for example what you love about your future self, and what you are curious about. Each time it may be different; there is no right or wrong. You are getting a feel for what your future holds. This allows for your most authentic self to surface. When I faced resistance in this exercise, I had to ask all those skeptical parts of myself to move aside, to let me experience it myself. Sure enough, these parts of me let me recognize there was "self" inside of me that felt lost. I just needed to display love, compassion, and patience, to find her!

Remember, "Know" is head knowledge, "Believe" is heart understanding, and "Do" is the action when both the mind and heart align. So, all this work is about alignment, getting ourselves in tune with the most authentic version of ourselves, so we can live abundant, fulfilling, significant lives. "Whole-life excellence" is a phrase I love to use!

READER REFLECTIONS

Write down your "I cannot" statements: I will not, I did not, I have not, it's not for me. Break them apart using the lenses:

What were you told?

What did you learn?

What did you experience?

What did you believe to be your truth?

Now look at your belief and reframe it to be empowering. There is a story under all of them; it is time to find your story and break it apart, so you can have freedom.

Be sure to journal your findings from your "future self" exercise.

Chapter Eight: Money and Emotions

"Money usually represents so much more than dollars and cents. It is tied to our deepest emotional needs: for love, power, security, independence, control, self-worth."

–Olivia Mellan

This chapter originated as a podcast. I had a sleepless night with other ideas about what I should share. Gratefully, I have a notepad and pen beside my bed because when my brain decides to fire it is on all cylinders, my friends, and it is chaos! Here is a foundational topic about emotions. Do they not rule the important decisions of our lives? They have MASSIVE implications on how you and I live day to day, in every area. Stay with me if this sounds foreign, I have a story to share.

Two years back, I had an event, and I was excited. It was taking me a shit load of courage to share on a mic at my local church. Kind of a big deal, so I invited my three precious kids (at the time, they were not so lovely, just saying, lol) to come with me. They sat at the table working on their homework. They looked up at me, and said, "Mom, can we stay home and just work on our homework?" Okay, so off I went, by myself. The event was great and went off without a hitch.

In contrast, though, driving home, I was a storm in the making. I got in the door and ensured the kids could hear me. I then proceeded to tidy up. What I was doing was smashing things around; well, not *smashing*, but you know when you are mad, the dishes just make more noise. So, here I was, loading the dishwasher with aggression. Would you know that it got my kid's attention? My daughter piped up: "What is your deal, Mom?" The waterworks began—mine. You know, the "ugly cry," where snot is dripping and you snort, while mascara runs down your face? As I cried, I tried to get the words out: "You did not show up for me, and I showed up for you. I am at every hockey game, ringette, and cheer. You name it. I am there. Do I want to be there? Sometimes I do not, I am tired, and I still do it. I am your biggest cheerleader, and I love you. Would it kill you to be there for me?" By this time, my daughter is like a deer in the headlights and wishing she had said nothing. Do you know what she said to me? "You have never needed anyone, Mom, let alone us, and you do not ask for help; you are always strong, and you don't show emotion."

All this time, when I was faking it till, I made it—holding it all together, being strong, not showing emotion, not asking for help—I thought that I was sheltering my kids. Why did I do this? Upon reflection, I have always done this. I grew up in a family where they swept things under the rug. I love my parents to pieces and that is what they taught me. For many reasons, we did not talk about our emotions; we did not let others know we were struggling or needed help— for fear of looking weak or no one needing to understand our business. We put on a mask and pretended all was well. I have lived my life not knowing how to talk about feelings, living in perfectionism, not asking for help, and *acting* like I've got my shit figured out.

Now, fast forward a couple of years, to 2020. I was reading the book *Permission to Feel*, by Mark Brackett. Do you know that emotions play a prominent role in our decision-making skills? Anyone who has read this book knows there is a chart of emotions and feelings at the back of the book, to help articulate what is going on within your body. I found this very insightful, and it gave me an idea. I found a chart and the steps that lead to emotional intelligence and made my way to Staples, a local print shop. I handed it to the lady and said, "Can you please zoom in on these and laminate them. I need five." The sweet lady looks at me and says, "You must be a teacher." I chuckle. Ummm, nope. "Oh, are you a mom of young children?" Then I laughed and even snorted a little. I told her that I am a mom of three teenagers, seventeen, fifteen, and eleven, plus a husband at the time, and myself, that needed those charts. She started to laugh and thought I was joking. Bless her heart, lol. She wished me luck, and as I was at the register ready to pay, I noticed a deck of cards there, with knock-knock jokes. I thought to myself, "This is perfect. I will introduce the chart to everyone and have a little family meeting, and to finish it off, give them jokes to lighten the blow."

Think about this for a second: were you taught how to label your feelings? I am not talking about happy, sad, good, fine, or stressed. I am talking about recognizing the more profound feelings and where they come from. If you already did—sweet, you are ahead of me! What can I say? I did not recognize this myself or teach my kids to openly talk about feelings and dive into the junk behind them. Deep down, I feared what would surface.

I challenge you to think about *your* decisions. Was there an emotion that drove a particular outcome? Here are some examples: emotional eating, retail therapy, and other numbing behaviors. For me, it was Facebook and, at one point, dating, to be honest. My financial decisions during our grieving cycle were driven by emotion: vacations, shopping, vehicles, jewelry—anything that would help to mask the feelings of abandonment, unworthiness, isolation, sadness, and jealousy. My list is long. I have lived it, trust me; this is likely why I am in this space, giving purpose to my pain and helping others reach financial freedom and wholeness.

My Jeep purchase was an emotional purchase. As I recall, we were on holiday visiting my parents in Ontario. I was sitting in the parking lot of a grocery store in my mom-mobile, which was a Honda Pilot, with my three kids in the back seat. This guy came speeding into the parking stall beside me. With his blonde beach waves blowing in the wind, he had a charisma and youthfulness about him. This was an older gentleman in his late fifties. If you have not guessed, it was a Jeep—the top down and doors off. I felt a sense of freedom, watching him step out onto the pavement. "Ugh," I thought to myself, "*I* want freedom and youthfulness." I liked what he had. Remember, I was on vacation, visiting my parents out east. The next day, I made my way to the dealership and traded my Honda Pilot in. True story. I refer to that as my "midlife crisis moment"—wanting to feel young again. When it came time to load up the vehicle with three kids, a dog, and all our belongings, back to Alberta, the Jeep did NOT have the same storage that a Honda Pilot has. Eeek! We can make poor financial decisions because of emotions. Decisions can be good or bad based on feelings, how we parent, and our performance at work. It is all intertwined.

One afternoon, when I was building material for a group of women, my then-husband looked over and said, "Why don't you include men?" I arrogantly chuckled. I then told him, "Men aren't willing to talk about money. We go deep and talk about emotions, identity, and stuff." He was not so happy with me and challenged me. I sat with this for a couple of days and realized that I was painting men with one paintbrush! Through the lens of what I grew up hearing, what was demonstrated in my surroundings, and past relationships, I believed that men do not talk about money and emotions. When in fact, that was not true. I was acting out a narrative I made up, based on my lens of experiences. I was humbled in that moment and decided to interview a bunch of men to get the truth. We must always learn to be detectives in search of the truth.

I did a blog on men, money, and emotions, from my findings. Turns out, we are not that different; the main difference is that women are given a landscape to have these discussions more often than men. The same fears, worries, and thoughts exist in both men and women.

However, they can show up differently in our patterns and our behaviors. I hope this gives some insight that you are not alone. We all have shame, embarrassment, and fear. No matter what race, gender, or lifestyle we come from, every one of us has a money story.

Throughout life, we may experience shame, guilt, embarrassment, or fear around money. The whole purpose of understanding your very own money story, which is uniquely yours, is that you can kick negative associations to the curb and replace them with the truth. So many people shared that they feel held hostage, due to old money decisions that prevent them from moving forward. Every financial decision that we make has a ripple effect.

Emotionally connected people have better finances. Let us take it even further: they make better husbands, wives, parents, employees, and well, humans. When we master our emotions, we can master our money, enhance our relationships, parent stronger, raise emotionally intelligent kids, perform better, and live authentic, whole-life excellence. Emotionally connected humans have a wholeness about them. Who does not want that?

Let me ask you, what do you hide behind? What is *your* crutch?

Patterns in your life—it is time we unpack them. I am a runner, and there was a season in my life when I ran over 130 miles in a month. I had to ask myself, why I was running that much? It was my way of escaping my life and trying to suppress my feelings, so I pounded it out on the pavement. Now, you may be thinking that is healthy, and I assure you it was not. I was not doing it for the joy of running anymore. I was doing it as a form of control and getting my happy endorphins when I was a hot mess. I pushed myself so hard that I was injured for six months and could not run at all! I became a monster; my kids can vouch for me! All because I did not recognize the emotional mess I was in. Running was my poison. What is your poison? Is it food, alcohol, drugs, sex, pornography, scrolling on social media, or retail therapy? We all have addictions—to avoid or gain a feeling that we are not getting somewhere else more fulfilling.

I used to have a sticky note on my pantry door that said, "Amie, are you hungry or is it an emotion?" Damn, every time I read that at the pantry door, I realized it was an emotion. As a result, I could step away from food and label what I was feeling. We must go further than labeling our feelings. We must get to the nitty gritty that is under the emotion. There is a story there that you can uncover. We carry junk in our trunks—my kids hate when I say that, but hell, it is true. These things weigh us down, impact our mental health, physical health, emotional health, and spiritual health.

POWER IN A PAUSE EXCERCISE

Here is a challenge for you: take a piece of paper and write down a significant decision that you have made. Break it down into categories: financially, relationally, and professionally. Ask yourself, why did it surface? How did you manage it? Was there an emotion that led to your reaction? What is under that emotion? Now, if you do that with one hundred percent radical responsibility and ownership, ask yourself how your best self would have moved forward, when faced with that decision. Can you look back and recognize a pattern or a thread, where you do it often?

All this happens subconsciously and fast. So how do we slow it down? We take a deep breath when we recognize an emotion surfacing, and this is the "pausing moment." Count down: five, four, three, two, one. Try to understand why you are feeling this way and what it truly means. Now, it is time to label the emotion and put it into words. Sometimes, journaling helps. Deliberately take the time to dig deep and find where the root of the problem comes from.

When we uncover things, we must ask ourselves if what we just learned is the truth or a lie. In recent years, a wide range of studies have found that third-person self-talk can improve emotional regulation and self-control by facilitating self-distancing and reducing egocentric bias. It is true; there is science behind it! We should be positively talking to ourselves in third-person narrative. It is helpful to reframe our feelings and bring our best selves to the table. How would *your* best self see this? Consider the money you will save on retail therapy and food costs. Your finances will improve, your relationship with loved ones will be enhanced, and your work performance will reach new heights, as your emotional intelligence increases. To drive this message home, let me share a recent story about how these types of thoughts impact our kids.

I have asked for permission to share this story, out of respect for the vulnerability that it takes, and the courage, to own our crap. Let me lay the foundation: we were a newly blended family, and there was tension. My vehicle needed repair and was out of commission, so I asked to borrow my daughter's car. My daughter, who has hard feelings towards my partner, shares that she is okay if I use her car to get groceries; however, she is not comfortable with him being in her car. She told me it was *her* car, which was a boundary she was putting in place. You can imagine all sorts of things coming up in me, and I was like a volcano inside, about to erupt.

I looked at her and said, "Okay, this is your boundary. I will respect that, and I will not use your car. I will get a cab or find another way, and I will ask for a time out from this conversation," as I knew that I was about to blow and did not want to say something I would regret. My feelings were intense; I needed to pause. So, I pulled the time out card and went to my room, as I was hurt, upset, and saddened by the complexity. I was disappointed that she could not see how this was playing out and affecting me. Time passed, and my sweet gal dug deep, discovering her true feelings behind all of this. She did not want him to have more time with me than he already did, and this was how she could control it. She was tired of sharing her momma and felt like she was losing her connection and time with me. Even though that was not the reality. After all, she was busy working and not using her car if I was borrowing it. She was able to label her emotions as jealousy and fear and concluded that they had nothing to do with the vehicle at all. She was crying and laughing, as she felt embarrassed that it was something so dumb.

Our feelings and emotions are never dumb, though they may seem irrational at times. When we unpack them, we can find the root. All of this allowed my daughter to bring her best self to the table and say, "Mom, I am sorry, and I love you. You can use my car as you see fit, and he can help you get groceries. I know that I am not losing time with you and that you will always be available for me." We can be very irrational when emotions surface; this was a splendid example—a proud mom moment for me, to watch my daughter process such deep, intertwined emotions, in real time.

This story shows that a lie drove my daughter's emotions, under everything. Emotions can be big, they surface fast, and we need to be able to sense, recognize, understand, label, express, and regulate them. Our breathing changes, our heart rate elevates, we have sweaty palms, restlessness, and irritability. Everyone experiences emotions differently. Learn how emotions show up for you. Identify your triggers or what activates you, and remember, it is okay to take a time out. As I took the time out, I wondered if this was just me trying to rug-sweep and suppress what was happening. I was at a loss as to how to move forward when I was in the thick of the chaos. I am grateful she was willing to unpack her true feelings. It takes bravery and courage to be so vulnerable, and freedom is on the other side.

Looking back, I realized this would have never happened, had I not brought home those emotional charts. So, as funny as they seemed and for all the resistance they gave me, it paid off. It helped build each one of us into better humans. I am constantly evolving; I am showing and sharing with my kids that I need to figure things out, too. As they watch me use these charts (found in the back of Mark Brackett's book, *Permission to Feel*), they, too, are implementing them. We are a work in progress, developing our skills personally and professionally. Trust me, when I say our kids are watching—more is caught, than taught.

Can you say, with confidence, that you have emotional intelligence? Are you instructing your kids like this? Emotional intelligence is a big buzzword right now, and for a good reason. Emotions impact all areas of your life. So, get on this growth-journey towards emotional healing and wellness. It is worth repeating, that emotionally connected people live better lives. They have better finances, live healthier lives, and experience life on a different level. So, are you ready to level up, my friends? It is time we master our emotions so we can master our lives and reach whole-life excellence, in all areas.

This next quote is a perfect addition to this chapter as we unpack our deepest emotional needs. "Money usually represents so much more than dollars and cents. It is tied up with our deepest emotional needs: love, power, security, independence, control, self-worth." –Olivia Mellan

We all have emotional needs for love, safety, security, and autonomy. We all need to feel seen, known, and understood. When any of these are out of alignment, so is our money. Let us dive deeper into love and money: who has, or knows, someone who has used money to find or gain love? Who comes from a family where others have tried to buy love? Maybe you have used money yourself, to buy your kids time and attention? People marry for money and lose who they are, all for the love of money. We can have healthy and unhealthy attachments to love and money; we need to self-reflect on the emotions behind our decisions. What are the driving factors?

Let us talk about money and power. In my house, I have called this a superiority complex. Money was a big issue in my second marriage, which ended, and we became one of the statistics. The power imbalance was a major contributor, along with money-infidelity. At first, I thought it was just him who had a money-superiority complex. He made good money, and it was often thrown around as a form of control. The more time I took to heal *my* money wounds and unpack *my* money story, I realized, "Damn! I, too, have a money-superiority complex." However, mine was different. Let me explain and you will see how money-superiority and power can show up in our romantic relationships and with our family members.

My story is one of being widowed at thirty-two, with three young kids. I remarried back in 2019. I married for love; he came into the marriage with nothing but a bicycle—we often joked about it; it was a wound, an insecurity that I never paid much attention to. Hindsight is always 20/20. His previous divorce had him starting over. I never looked down upon his situation, but I held myself above it, as I had two houses, a decent vehicle, and money saved for retirement. It was never his intention to make me feel as though *he* was superior due to his substantial salary, and it was not *my* intention to make him feel as though I was superior, in terms of assets. Each of us had our lenses that played a role in the stories we told ourselves. We then would seek to justify our beliefs, which were not true. We can do things subconsciously and consciously that can cause hurt and wounds to the people we love the most. As we did.

Communicating about money was hard for us. I have a whole chapter on this, later in the book. You get to learn from my mistakes, lucky you. Openly discussing your emotions around money, love, power, security, independence, and self-worth, is key to a healthy partnership. Learn one another's money story, as this is what feeds the lies we believe and solidifies our belief systems. Until we break apart these lies, we will not be able to reach financial wholeness for ourselves, or as a unit.

My money language is security through-and-through. I long for, and look for, security. It all circles back to my own money story, my experience of life shattering, and losing everything. When I feel pressure regarding financial security, I become a gremlin. It is as if I do not even recognize myself anymore, anxiety, fear, shame, and embarrassment are front and center. My emotions surface, and I can run every scenario known to man and believe it will happen to us.

My desire to be secure is at my core. For most moms, I think this is true. This need for financial security sends us into a loop when we face a financial crisis. Working through my money-security, I have had to be intentional about what I can and cannot control. From my own experience, I know that the financial pressure of providing can also fall on our partners. They feel the need to provide and give stability when that is challenged. It can affect all aspects of their self-worth, identity, and so forth.

Did you know that money was this complex? Financial security can mean different things to different people. It implies stability—my children will have the best chance at growing up with a decent number of opportunities (not spoiled but not left to their own devices, either). I like the middle ground. It means not worrying about paying bills, food, or emergencies that may pop up. It means less stress. I know I have had seasons in my life where I have put too much emphasis on financial security and, sometimes, not enough. In my experience, there is a middle ground. It requires me to get to the core of who I am and what I value, to look at what I can control and what I cannot and getting clear on my future goals. It would be beneficial if you did similar exercises to break free from the power of money and the security it can have on you.

Next, let's look at independence. We want to experience autonomy *and* belonging. How do we do that with our money and our relationships? It can seem like a paradox, and in all reality, it is about understanding the emotions behind wanting each piece of the pie. Why do we want a sense of independence? Why do we want to feel included? How do we have both and what that might look like, are the million-dollar questions. Every person must have a little money. This will look different to everyone, and this is where I guide people to start. Have a credit card in your name and a bank account with money in it; you determine what works for your situation. I suggest this because you want to have built up a banking history. Have a credit score, so that if something happens, such as a death, separation, or divorce, you would have at least built up a record with the banks and have money available to you, instantly.

To be clear, this all needs to be done with transparency with your partner and explained in a way that does not give the impression of having a "plan B." My reasoning for this is that it was as if my identity and all my bank history went with Bart when he passed away. We were high school sweethearts and thought that by doing everything jointly, we were doing things according to the book. We were becoming one and "adulting." We did not know that when finances are joint: they only build history and credit scores for the primary account holder, which was my husband. When I say he took our credit score and banking history to the grave, he sure did. Now, the banks were telling me I had to apply for a credit card and a mortgage. It was as if I had been invisible to the banks for sixteen years. Talk openly with one another about this, so it is received well and not perceived as a form of control. Another of our basic needs, in life and money, is a sense of control.

I think to myself at times, about the song by Carrie Underwood, "Jesus Take the Wheel". I had prayed for that, many times. It is crazy to think about our need for control. I have fallen into this, and it made me crazy. When things are stressful, my controlling nature hits an all-time high; my sympathetic nervous system goes into fight-or-flight mode. We can use money to gain control over things we want. It is an illusion that we can control everything—the only thing we do have control over, is our actions.

I was reading an article in *Forbes Magazine*, that indicated control is keeping track of mistakes.

- Control is judging progress or completed tasks.

- Control is looking at others' actions from a happy vs. unhappy standpoint of how it serves self.

- Control is giving to get something, manipulating circumstances to go your way.

- Control is a lack of trust in others to make sound financial decisions.

- Control kills intimacy with your partner in all forms, including your money.

- Control breaks apart your relationship with children.

We need to learn to manage money by managing cash, by failing and getting it wrong, so our children know how to get it right. As parents, we are not sure we can help micromanage our kids and their finances. We must educate, equip, and empower them to make wise decisions. Allow them to build character development; the same is true within relationships. We will get it wrong, and we are imperfect beings. So, how can you grow and learn and do better, going forward?

Because we already covered limiting beliefs, we know thoroughly that our self-worth can be tied to money. Our identity is warped by how much we make, the titles associated with our names, the positions we hold, and our net worth. This is why I think Olivia Mellan's quote is so powerful, it speaks the truth: that our emotions around money are tied to love, power, security, independence, control, and self-worth.

DISMANTLE EXCERCISE

When we look at our need for love, power, security, independence, and self-worth, we see our lenses that make up the core of who we are from what we were told, learned, experienced, and how we formulated our beliefs. Soon this will be rolling off your tongue, which will be wonderful. You will then be able to recognize and reflect faster on how, where, and why, obstacles are showing up in your money and life.

All of this is formulated through your money story, narrated by using the lenses:

What were you told about love and money?

What did you learn about love and money?

What did you experience about love and money?

What is your belief? Is it true? What is true?

What were you told about money and security?

What did you learn about money and security?

What did you experience when it came to money and security?

What is your belief? Is it true? What is the truth?

What were you told about money and independence?

What did you learn about money and security?

What did you experience when it came to independence and money?

What is your belief? Is it true? What is the truth?

What were you told about money and your self-worth?

What did you learn about money and your self-worth?

What is your experience with money and self-worth?

What belief do you have? Is it true? What is the truth?

I bring you all these questions regarding the lenses, for you to dig deep and realize that we all have emotions, limiting beliefs, and money stories hindering our financial future. When we do this work, we can recognize the stories underneath. From there we can go back to the "Five R's":

Recognize It: Call it out—what it is, what you are feeling, and where in the body.

Reflect: Where is this feeling coming from? What is the underlying reason it surfaced?

Rebuke It/Refuse It: It is not the truth. It is a lie; reject the thought.

Reframe It: Write out an empowering belief that cancels out the lie. Stay curious and ask yourself, what if I am wrong? What is possible? How is this belief serving me, and what could be different?

Reposition Yourself: Speak out the empowering belief, repeatedly—there is power in mantras. Live out differently, by doing one thing that brings you closer to your future self.

Changing our thoughts leads to changing our actions. We may have lived a good portion of our lives in certain patterns, behaviors, and belief systems. It may get uncomfortable as we embark on topics and stories and uncover past parts or even current hurts or wounds we carry.

The goal in all of this is not for you to relive your trauma, wounds, or hurt. This work aims to hold what is possible in one hand and break things down in the other hand. Though it sounds contradictory you can experience both simultaneously. Living through your lenses to this point, you have done the best you could. Honour that part of yourself that has done the work. Now that you *know* better you can go even further. That, my dear one, is why you are reading this book. You are kicking ass, my friend, and your future self will thank you!

READER'S REFLECTIONS

What has surprised you? What have you uncovered? Remember, if anything is too overwhelming, I encourage you to seek professional help from a counselor, therapist, or doctor. You need to take care of yourself in the best conceivable way and hold compassion for yourself, kindness, and love. You, my dear one, have been through so much, and you are still standing. You got this, and I am here with you. You can use my mantra, "I ducking got this," if it helps!

Chapter Nine: Fear & Finances

"Fear is a manipulative emotion that can trick us into living a boring life"

–Donald Miller.

Fear is at an all-time high, in today's world. Fear, in and of itself, is not bad; we all need and have, fear. Fear is designed to keep us safe. At the perception of threat, fear activates the sympathetic nervous system and triggers an acute stress-response that allows our bodies to fight, flight, freeze, or fawn. Remember, as these responses kick in, the brain is flooded with stress hormones, such as adrenaline and cortisol. Fear is required in certain aspects of our lives; however at other times this fear response occurs when there is no danger or intense situation. This triggers anxiety. Understanding these responses and being aware of how to regulate them will increase your overall mental, physical, and emotional well-being.

Why does fear show up in our money? Our security is tied to money, and when something threatens that, our security and safety are affected. It can be the pandemic that has stricken fear in you, or a job loss, a separation, a divorce; many more life stressors can bring about this fear around finances—sending our nervous systems into distress. Our sense of reasoning is hijacked, as our body prioritizes survival, instead of creative problem-solving. I love what Bari Tessler says: "We can't think our way out of feelings! The best we can do is say hello to them, calm ourselves down, and stay gentle with ourselves as we allow our feelings to move through."

It is not always about how much money you have but how secure you feel with the money you have. I am going to repeat this. It is not about how *much* you have or make; it is about what you *do* with what you have and the feelings of security it brings you. I had an "aha moment", there is an enormous difference. Fear of our finances is not always about lack of funds. It can be other things, a more generalized anxiety about our money or anxiety about numbers and math. It can be a feeling of unpreparedness or not understanding all the terms and acronyms: fear of looking stupid, incompetent, embarrassed, ashamed, or envious.

Common financial fears:

- Feeling of never being able to get out of debt.

- Not understanding financial concepts or terms.

- Crippling fear of job loss.

- Discussing money with a partner.

- Risks of not being able to work.

- Having to declare bankruptcy.

- Not being able to retire and having to work the rest of one's life.

- Having to support elderly parents.

Our fears cause stress, and this stress has an impact on our physical, emotional, and mental well-being. So, how do we face these fears, anxieties, and worries about money, head on? Our natural tendency is to avoid it altogether. I call this "money avoidance." The minute we feel anxiety or worry, we release that pressure by avoiding the situation, topic, or task.

Here is a notable example: A couple knew it was time to put a financial roadmap in place, and they were excited to start. When it came time to gather all their documents, suddenly, resistance reared its ugly head—she began to feel embarrassed and ashamed of their habits and patterns. One partner was okay sharing but the other was paralyzed with fear of someone else knowing about their personal money situation—as if it was a dirty little secret. (We all have done stupid shit with our money; you are not alone!) So, right away, she stopped the process. It brought up uncomfortable emotions that she was not sure how to work through, avoidance. This elevated her feelings of anxiety and worry. This approach does not help, as it leaves us in the same spot as we started. If you do what you have always done, you will get what you have always gotten. Had she gathered all the documents, brought them to a professional, and said, "OMG, I faced resistance when gathering these documents. What does this mean?" The outcome could have started her on the path to financial wholeness sooner rather than later. Live out your money, differently.

Self reflection has power, it brings light, and shame cannot live where there is light. Shame no longer has power over us. The fear drops away, and then we can have an open and honest conversation about the stories hindering our financial future. Doing this brings the power to break away fear, anxiety, and worry. Does it take courage and bravery to be so bold as to say that? YES! What is needed to become financially whole is transparency, freedom, and a roadmap that will bring you peace of mind because you have a plan. This approach to money brings healing. Will we still have setbacks and trip-ups? The answer is YES, as I have said before, no one is immune to financial fears. The goal is to be able to nip it in the bud, before it can derail you or start firing up all your old, limiting beliefs.

Being afraid of our finances can be crippling. I know firsthand, as I have been there and we sometimes stay stuck for longer than we care to admit. Too many people have "an ostrich with its head in the sand," approach towards money. But ignoring your finances will hurt you. It is time to take inventory of the numbers and any emotional and limiting beliefs you hold, underneath your experiences with money.

Here are common responses to fear around money:

- Resistance to thinking or talking about money.

- Withdrawing from activities due to financial stress.

- Being obsessed with counting cash or checking accounts, multiple times a day.

- Refusing to touch money.

- Depression and physical ailments.

- Fear of failure, fear of success.

Let us talk about this fear of failure and what failure means. I wish to shift your perspective on failing—if you did not try, you would not have failed. You had the courage and bravery to show up in your arena, not knowing your odds. So, why do we get so deflated by the thought that we have failed?

Here is how I see it: failing is a beautiful thing, yet, so often, when I fail, I *am* a failure. But here is the difference: one is a "who", and the other is a "do". We need to be sure they each stay in their lane. So, if you fail, it means something you tried did not end the way you had thought; that is the "do", not *who you are as a person*. Stay with me on this, the "who" is who you are as a person. Just because we do not succeed at the "do", doesn't mean we *are* the "do"—in this case, a failure. It is quite the opposite, you see. As we learn and grow from our setbacks, they become our setups. I'll say that again: *our setbacks become our setups*. We develop new and better ideas from lessons learned from failing at something. When fear stops us, we stop trying. It paralyzes us, as we run with lies in our minds, telling us we cannot do something or how others say it will be perceived. This list can be life changing to your future.

How do we embrace our fears? We press on anyway, knowing that if we fail, we can recognize our strengths through our weaknesses. We learn what attributes need our attention or skill development. Let's grow our confidence, give, and receive feedback which will boost our ability to try again and get it right or pivot and prosper. Being in the arena ourselves builds our compassion for others when they face setbacks. We need to give that same compassion and extend it to ourselves.

You may have to go first, to create space to talk openly with others about money, even within your safe network. Scary thought, right? To be honest, we are all scared to go first. We all face similar challenges and struggles—we have common emotions regarding money. When we share, it breaks down stigma and builds community. When we realize we are not alone, we can hold each other accountable with constructive feedback, out of love for one another, and encouragement, to flourish and thrive.

SETBACKS TO SET UPS EXERCISE

Celebrate your fear, as it shows you care about what is in store for you. Embrace it when you fail or fall flat on your face because at least you showed up. Be bold and brave; what matters most is what you do when you are down. Get back up! Remember that ownership is solely on you;

no one can want it more than you want it for yourself. Circle the obstacles or saboteurs that affect you:

- **Unhealthy Beliefs:** What are you telling yourself about the fears you have about money and your future?

- **Lack of Purpose:** Are you feeling a lack of vision, clarity, or direction for your financial future?

- **Inconsistent Boundaries:** What boundaries do you have to protect your mental, emotional, physical, and financial well-being?

- **Naysayers:** People in your circle that are dream crushers or Negative Nancys, that affect your money or people draining your finances.

- **Out of Balance:** Self-reflection on where you are off kilter. Sometimes, this is not enough margin in all areas of our lives or even a hormonal imbalance that requires attention.

When our bodies give us emotions or physical feelings, think of them as an alarm bell ringing, telling you something is wrong. It is your job to investigate what is happening within your mind, body, and spirit to detect the gap or missing link that leads to whole-life excellence.

- **Lack of Belonging:** How are you using money to fill this void? Oh, snap! I have done this one a lot.

- **Depleted Bravery/Courage:** Lack of belief in yourself and your abilities; our minds are complex, and mindset matters.

- **Purpose:** Missing your spark—are you using your gifts to serve others?

- **Dimmed:** Feeling squashed or dimmed by outside influences.

- **Unhealthy Behaviors:** Look inward; how are you living out your best self?

When we can journal or self-reflect on these saboteurs that creep in, we can take inventory and make the necessary adjustments that are within our control.

PIVOT AND PROSPER EXERCISE

Those were our obstacles and let us draw attention to things we can control:

- **Readiness:** For instance, are you ready for your financial future? Do you have a plan? Can you articulate a vision board, a money road map?

- **Relationships:** Who is helping you get there? Have the right people on your damn bus: money coach, trusted advisor, accountant, lawyer.

- **Emotions:** Know that your feelings play a part and recognize them before they take over driving your finances.

- **Ownership:** One-hundred per cent radical responsibility for where you are currently in your finances and where you are going in your future.

- **Resources:** Who and what can you leverage to reach your financial goals? Financial literacy is massive; emotional intelligence is significant.

- **Balance:** Having a margin in all areas is vital. It would be best if you have balance in your diet, physical exercise, calendar, and sleep, so you are at your optimum performance.

- **Radiance:** Know your worth, have your money mantras, and live out the future self that you envision.

You have heard me say that there is more to money than numbers. However, we must first understand our relationship with money: money psychology, my wonderful peeps. You need to understand the intersection between your money story, your behaviors, and patterns, limiting beliefs, and the underlying root causes. All things work together to alleviate fear, worry, anxiety, and depression, to minimize our poor financial decisions.

Let's go back to the lenses through which we experience life:

What we were told.

What we learned.

What we experienced

What we formulated and believe to be the truth.

Our financial problems are not the result of us being lazy, stupid, or out in left field. Understanding your money psychology will help you understand your relationship with money. When you unpack this, it will make perfect sense how you have lived out your finances.

I am sure you are anxious as you wait for the other shoe to drop. We know that unexpected costs pop up and throw us into a financial loop. It can be a car repair, a water heater in the house, or a new roof. At times it can feel like there is always something lurking around every corner. Making sure to plan every month to put money aside is key to giving you peace of mind in the interim.

The thing with money is that no one is alike; we all have different hopes, dreams, fears, and insecurities. So, taking the time to get over your issues around money and learn how to make money work for you in a way that feels good, is the most important thing you can do for your self-care. You are your own financial superhero, and you have the power within. You must tap into it and build on it.

Fear in all forms can be incapacitating. It is a strong emotion that affects our frame of mind and controls our actions if we are not careful. Acknowledging the fear affecting your decisions is the first step to conquering it. Everything is intertwined; our well-being in body, mind, and spirit affects our decisions and emotions around money. So, how are you fueling these areas of your life? Is what you are doing decreasing the fear and anxiety about your finances, or increasing it?

EXPLORING TRUTH EXERCISE

Journaling about our money, our fears, and anxieties around money, is a great start. "Brain dump," as this gives you something to reflect on: write down what is worrying you and when you tend to experience these feelings. Be descriptive. Can you notice a pattern? When we put it on paper, we have the ability then to ask ourselves the four questions:

Byron Katie's Four Questions:

- Question 1: Is it true?

- Question 2: Can you absolutely know it is true?

- Question 3: How do you react—what happens—when you believe that thought?

- Question 4: Who would you be without the thought?

- Turn the thought around.

We have previously discussed the block between our "Know" and "Believe." However, I have found a helpful technique that I love taking my coaching clients through, to achieve financial healing, I implement somatic movement to release old patterns along with the emotional tapping technique paired with meditation. Check out our "Sharing the Manual" YouTube channel for resources.

When we think about the lies hindering our success, we need to break them apart. Tapping is an excellent way of acknowledging them, giving permission to feel them, uncovering where they came from, reframing them, and rewiring the truth—breaking down barriers between your head and your heart. Back to the Five R's: Recognize, Reflect, Rebuke/Reject, Reframe, and Reposition.

Acupressure points help to reduce stress and anxiety. I typically start above the eyebrow, side of the eye, under the eye, and under the nose, then to the chin, collarbone, under the arm, and top of the head. I work through these sets for each round. First, find what works for you. Then, check out our YouTube channel, "Tapping Money Emotions," as I walk you through the process.

We do five rounds. It is crucial to complete each step to get the full effects of this type of therapy. Understanding the five rounds:

- Recognizing the emotion and feeling and where it is showing up in your body. "Fear of not having enough."

- Reflecting on the emotion by allowing it to be present and feel it. "It's real and very present and crippling."

- Rebuke what is underneath the feeling and emotions, recognize the root cause of it? "I fear this because of the lies I believe about my self-worth and future." Release and let it go, as it is not the truth of who you are. "This is not my truth, and I will not let it cripple or define me."

- Reframe the wrong thought with the truth of who you are and how you will live out this newfound truth. "I am enough, and money will flow to me and through me."

- Reposition yourself with an empowerment statement.

Turning that negative thought around, we are rewiring your neurological pathways. Our thoughts lead the way; this is a fundamental technique to rebuild the neurological pathways that create a life without fear, anxiety, and depression—leading us to abundance, fullness, joy, and peace. I want that for you—for you to have financial wholeness, to release your old patterns and emotions and live out your truest calling.

READER REFLECTIONS

I hope you complete the last exercise and the following tips. That is how you will get the most out of this book, by applying the exercises and doing the inner work. You get out what you put into this journey.

Create a vision board, project your future self on your board, and "Be it till you become it." I love this phrase. It puts your willingness and openness to receive and live into the most authentic calling of yourself. Declare what is yours for the taking.

I wish I knew the mastermind behind this next saying, so I could send a thank you. I am sending you love and kindness for your generosity:

"I need my faith to conquer my fears, not my fear to conquer my faith."

Chapter Ten: Money Myths & Confessions

"I'm good at sticking to a budget when I have no money."

–said Every Woman.

Did anyone else laugh at this chapter's quotation? I sure did. You must love truth-bombs when they are thrown out effectively. I wanted to include this chapter because I know it impacted me and others when I shared it on a podcast. So, let us debunk some of the myths about money and what you have been waiting for... the nitty gritty confessions. I cannot tell you how blessed I am to have shared space with these remarkable individuals from all social classes, who let me into their emotions around money and openly and honestly shared their deepest, darkest secrets.

We are doing this, so you feel informed and empowered, so that you are not alone in this big, imperfect world of finances. There are other ideas out there for you to read, and hopefully, you get what you need right here in this book. I have also compiled a recommended reading list at the back of this book for you to continue your learning journey. I hope it inspires you to follow my social media platforms as I keep relevant material coming your way. My hope for you is that you will have the courage to open up in a whole new way when it comes to your money. You probably know it to be true that our emotions have tremendous power, both consciously and subconsciously. It is time to take back control.

We start with financial myths:

You Gotta Be Rich Myth

We have all heard of this myth. It would be best if you were rich to invest. FALSE. You can invest as little as fifty dollars per month, the minute you turn eighteen. Open those accounts, and every little bit counts. I love the line "power in the PAC (PAC meaning pre-authorized contribution plan)," it makes me think of Pacman. I know, I just dated myself once again, but that is quite all right. The more time you invest, the more it compounds and grows exponentially.

You're Too Old Myth

If you had a later financial start, you may believe this lie. I am in my fifties-it is too late to start investing. When you know better, you can do better. Better late than never. What money story are you believing? Do not have an ostrich head-in-the-sand approach to money. You can still position yourself for retirement at the youthful age of fifty. I know this to be true.

Timing The Market Myth

You make money by timing the market—buy low and sell high. This approach is a gamble; experts have been trying this for years and even they get it wrong. Be realistic when you are self-investing. I tell clients to have money invested with the professionals and then have play money of their own, so that if they lose it all, they will be okay.

Borrow To Make a Buck Myth

Have you heard of leveraging? *In other words, you borrow money from banking or other financial institutions to invest.* Word on the street is, that you will always be on top. WRONG! Leveraging, or borrowing money to invest, is a risky tactic. Unless you know what you are doing, do not put yourself at risk unless you are okay with losing money and still owing it back. Remember, sometimes money is not yours to lose. Debt mortgages your future. Be informed.

Growth In Savings Account Myth

This myth is relevant for young adults or older generations. *Keep your money in your savings to grow.* Here are some facts: your average savings account is less than one per cent return, and inflation is, on average, two to three per cent, unless we are in a pandemic. That moves you backward. Invest that money in your savings account, in a better investment vehicle. Choose an investment account that matches your risk tolerance and gets your money working for you. It is worth noting that if you are scared to lose money in the market, there are options to have guarantees built into your portfolio. All you need to do is ask. Educate yourself and get the right people on your team of advisors.

Tax Refund Wish List Myth

I have fallen into this next myth, if I am honest, even a couple of times:

Spend your tax refund. NO. NO. NO. The goal should be to earn more and save more. Using your tax refund for lifestyle purchases is dangerous. When we make more money, we spend more; however, if you do not have an established emergency fund, here is a great opportunity to use some of your tax refund to build that up. Put it into an investment that is liquid-able (readily available in a moment's notice), just in case. Think "long-term savings" and protect yourself from the unexpected detours that life can throw at you.

Lease or Buy Myth

This next myth is no secret. *Financing and leasing a vehicle are the way to go.* Let us call it what it is. A new car is a depreciating asset: we drive it off the lot and are hit with a considerable decrease in value. When we say "yes" to something, we may need to say "no" to something else, later. Do you want this commitment for the next five or ten years? It is necessary to pay attention to the actual cost of the vehicle. Did you calculate the interest throughout your term commitment, so you can make an informed decision as to whether that makes sense? Heads up, avoid the dealerships that take your current vehicle debt and put it on your new purchase. I have seen this myth burn many people financially with an insurance claim, be aware.

I Got Approved Myth

Debt is a tool...NOT. Society pushes it upon us at such a young age that normalize car loans, student debt, and consumer debt. We love those retail cards from The Brick or The Bay. Living below your means is better and paying cash for things you want. Do not get caught in the hustle of purchasing. You will be stuck in the hustle to work more and more. Many people, through my interviews, called these debts "traps." What you water, grows. I'll let you ponder that saying.

The Bigger the Better Myth

This may challenge you; if you are like me and like being challenged. Here it goes: *Conquer large debt first.* This is not always the smartest decision. What are your thoughts? Review your debt and interest rates on everything. You will want to tackle your highest-interest debt first. But there is also something to be said about hammering out small debt, as it can be a quick win and keep the momentum going. Doing this gives us a sense of progress and keeps us motivated. Have an advisor help you if you are unsure.

No Job No Need Myth

Who has heard this one? *A stay-at-home parent does not need life insurance.* This one got me fired up. I remember having a discussion with my late husband. He would need a cook, cleaner, chauffeur, grocery shopper, full-time nanny, and so much more, to replace me. He laughed and the next thing you knew, I had a million-dollar policy on myself. Unfortunately, we did not calculate his need correctly. Unfortunately, hindsight is 20/20. If only I knew what I know now, I would have been a millionaire. Properly protect your family from the risks in life, including your children. Talk to a trusted advisor today.

Credit Good/Bad Myth

This next myth can be contradictory: *Stay away from credit card debt.* Credit cards are the gateway to increased debt, but they also have a plus-side of building your credit score. Having a good credit score (a score indicating your ability to fulfill your financial commitments based on your financial history) helps you when you wish to purchase your first home. There is a right and wrong way to manage your credit cards. Credit cards also can give rewards such as points or cash-back incentives. Use accordingly. Please pay attention to what cards you have and why you have them. I like to hold two credit cards; I don't carry a balance on either. The key is to pay it off *every month*. Have one with a small limit; this one is more of an emergency card in case your other one does not work or is compromised. The main one I use for all my purchases within the month. I do this to collect points and so I can eventually travel for free. Using a credit card correctly helps your credit score and provides other incentives. A little reminder is to be sure to have a credit card in your name, so *you* are building up *your* credit score. Being a joint holder does not count towards your score. I learned that the hard way.

It's On Sale Myth

Oh, this one is great. Are you ready?

It is on sale, buy-one-get-one, or buy three for ten dollars. This gets people all the time. If you do not need the extra, then it is not worth it. So often, these deals are consumer trap. My kids always say this to me on Fridays, our grocery day: "Mom, they are three for ten dollars!" If it is red and white chips, then yes, we do need the three bags; anything else, we do not. My weakness is Old Dutch nacho chips are red and white. It must be said that I eat three bags over the weekend, but I only eat the red chips and no they do not just sell the red chips. Did I help my case or make it worse? OMG, I am laughing as I type this out. I tell the kids when we are at the till, to watch the price. The item was three for ten dollars, but we only got one; sure enough, it rang in at $3.33, when scanned. The kids were shocked that we got the sale price and did not even have to buy three. Be wise with your purchases and use them as teachable moment that things are not always as they seem. Do the math, pay attention, and only buy what you need. Live within your means.

Work More Pay More Myth

When I was younger, I heard these words from my folks, yes, they bought into this myth. *Working harder means more money.* Who else can relate to that one? Yet again, it is false. I love demonstrating to my kids that working smarter pays excellent rewards. Hustling is overrated. Building out margin (I call this space or breathing room) in all areas of our lives is so important. Know your worth, and charge accordingly. As I say that, I know women, including myself, who get hung up on a saboteur/imposter syndrome visit, over that topic. You may have to go back to some inner work and find the story underneath your self-worth—I often do.

When I listed my house for sale, people kept asking me where I would go. I could not precisely answer that; my goal has always been "mountains and water". Time will tell. I casually say, "I am not worried about finding a place to rent." Next thing you know, everyone in my circle has an opinion!

Must Buy Myth

Which leads us beautifully into the next myth: *Buying is better than renting.* Renting has always had a stigma about it, of throwing your money away or paying someone else's mortgage instead of building your equity and having an asset. Remember that owning a home also means less flexibility, plus —high insurance costs, repairs, taxes, and more. I have moved a lot, and I have learned through experience that if you do not intend to stay at any house/location for more than three to five years, it does not make sense to buy. Do what is best for you, and do not listen to others' opinions about renting or buying. It is your job to disappoint as many people as possible, as long as you do not disappoint yourself. Silence the noise of the world, society, friends, and relatives. Stick to trusting your inner knowledge about what is best for you and your family.

Show Me the Money Myth

We are nearing the end of our money myths, and we have three more for you: *Salary positions pay better than hourly.* This is another risky misconception. It all depends on the number of hours worked. Be sure to do the math. Before taking on any position, research, get the job description, and set clear expectations for your work week. Running such calculations give you the advantage of making an informed decision and setting clear expectations.

No Go Years Myth

AHHHH, this is not always true:

Your cost of living will be lower in retirement. Typically, the cost of groceries, insurance, healthcare, and utilities *increase,* along with inflation. I advise couples to work through my worksheet, "Shedding Light on Retirement." It has questions for you and your partner to get a feel for what your reality will be in your retirement years. Head on over to my website and email me a request at www. sharingthemanual.ca; I call it the Retirement Checklist. Even when you are younger, it is a must-have, as it helps navigate discussions with your partner about the future.

You can never start talking about your financial future at too young an age. The younger, the better; be proactive versus reactive.

Invincible Myth

Finally: *I don't need disability insurance.* Many of us think we are invincible and that nothing will happen to us. The truth is that one in three people in their twenties will become disabled. The stats don't lie. Over 500,000 Canadians per week are off work, thirty percent due to mental health-related disability claims. Did you know that disability policies can cover this? Get informed, is all I have to say. Having a work policy is always a wise decision. However, check if there are gaps in the policy, whether your disability or life policy is taxable versus non-taxable, how long the pay period is, and what is and is not covered. It can be overwhelming to read the fine print and seek a professional to help make sense of the mess. Being educated, you can make informed decisions. You then have the power to set yourself up for your future. Some policies even give return of premium.

Money Confessions

Now let us talk about money confessions. I researched and interviewed many people to get an idea of some of the shame, guilt, and embarrassment of people's financial decisions. I, too, Googled money confessions, and they made me laugh. Here are my findings.

From online I read:

"I still go to my dad for financial advice."

"I make way more than my parents."

"I paid off my fiancés' debt."

"I am the poorest of my friends."

All I can say is WOW. Pretty surface level if you ask me. Thank you to the people I interviewed for getting real and honest about sharing their financial missteps. They took my research up a notch. Their honesty and bravery are admirable. Pay attention to the disclosures that resonate for you. Get your pen and paper ready.

"I am in constant overdraft."

"I secretly stash money away in a personal account in case my partner leaves."

"I feel I have to buy forgiveness from my partner."

"I am only staying married as I can't afford to leave; I need this lifestyle."

"I tell my partner to rein in their spending, but I don't."

"Thinking about money keeps me up at night; I hide the stress from my family."

"I always pay for dinner and drinks when out with friends, and I want them to like me and think I am doing well."

"I don't want to be at home, so I work like a dog, and I like the extra recognition and money; it fuels my ego."

"I make money; therefore, I have more value."

"Making money allows me to control people and things."

"I want the kids to choose me, so I use money as a tool and buy them things."

"I have opened up store credit cards without my partner knowing so I can buy things."

"I tell people we are fine when we are in financial trouble."

"I've had to declare bankruptcy because I choose not to rein in my spending."

"When I buy something on sale, I justify buying something for myself as I would have spent that money anyway."

I hope the above list has awakened you to your own thought or behaviour patterns. Self-reflection is a beautiful and helpful practice because it brings awareness and when we are aware, we can make changes.

Wait, there is more...

"I allude to having money to keep my friend group."

"I want to date that person, so I have given the illusion of money."

"I get irritated and jealous when my friends and family are doing well financially."

"I borrow money from my parents without my partner knowing."

"I hide my Amazon orders when they come in."

"I lie about what I spend money on."

I admire the courage that it took my interviewees to share with me. That I can relate to many of their confessions for sure. I used to hold a lot of shame, embarrassment, and judgment for using money in unhealthy ways. However, throughout my journey, I have learned that much of our spending is driven from within. When we are unwell on the inside, it will reflect on the outside— that is the heart of my message, dear ones. You are not alone in navigating the strain of finances. It is an inside job.

Many of our patterns and behaviours arise from our money stories and the lenses through which we do life. I have mentioned before that we wear lenses, and those lenses distort the truth. They can lead you astray, and it is time for you to reach financial wholeness. The only way to do that is to speak out your shame, guilt, fear, worries, and embarrassment about money. Share with a safe person who can help you dismantle and rewire your patterns, so you have control of your finances, and your finances stop controlling you. Get back in the driver's seat of your life so you can kick ass with your money!

UNPACKING EXERCISE

What are some money myths or confessions that you have been told?

Did you learn any myths throughout your years?

What have you experienced firsthand, like me?

Which myths do you need to unpack?

You can think of more myths we need to debunk, or you may have thoughts that need clarifying. Then, let us know what comes up for you so we can help others with similar experiences, opinions, or beliefs.

Remember, our thoughts become our actions, so we need to put intention into what our brains are thinking.

Know: head knowledge

Heart: heart understanding

Do: ability to live out when we are aligned.

READER REFLECTIONS

Write them down or try doodling—pen-to-paper is a form of expression. I have learned to let the pen and paper do its thing; sometimes, I journal, and sometimes, I doodle.

Did you know that we write differently or express ourselves differently with different emotions in our bodies? When I look back at my journal, there are pages where I write all capitals, other pages are small printing, and then a mix. At times I am single-spaced and then double-spaced. None of my expressions are consistent. When I put research behind it, I learned that this is our body's way of releasing emotion, with movement.

When I read my journal and notice my mood, there are often many spaces and giant letters. This typically shows up when I am upset or bothered by something. My more fluent, neat writing is when I am in a good place. It is a good thing you can't see my journals—they might alarm you, ha-ha.

Stay curious as to how you express yourself.

Chapter Eleven: Trauma Plays a Role

"If you want to be free of the trauma they caused you, you're going to have to forgive them, and yourself, for the whole experience."

–Morgan McKean

Easier said than done—did you know that something could be holding you back from financial freedom? Now, I am about to throw the "T" word out. Did you guess it is trauma? Trauma plays into our money. I have even heard it be called financial PTSD or Post Traumatic Stress Disorder. People have looked at me and said, "Amie, I do not have money trauma." I think, "Okay, let me throw things out that can or will shift your perspective on this." The T-word is presumed that anyone with trauma is fucked up or broken. You just heard a bold statement, and is that not the perceived truth of the stigma? I am not saying that it is the truth, but I have had my fair share of trauma in my life, and I know how others have treated me or looked at me.

There are many trauma categories: emotional, physical, sexual, and financial abuse. These traumas affect how we manage money. What matters is how we are viewing these traumas through the lenses of our own experiences which I discuss later in this chapter. Unfortunately, there is no shortage of abuse and trauma in our world. Money is not immune to this conversation.

Consider if you or anyone you know, has faced at least three months without adequate means to meet financial obligations due to illness, injury, or unemployment. Traumatic stress is the loss of a home, pandemic-related financial stress, business, or personal bankruptcy. That is TRAUMA right there, my peeps. People are in relationships with very destructive money behaviors, and many people can be affected, without even genuinely knowing the magnitude.

Trauma can be passed down generationally, relationally, societally, or systemically. We often rug-sweep it and pretend it was nothing. STOP IT, trauma *is* something, and it has the power to control your financial future, if it remains buried. It was said to me once that "buried feelings never die; they surface repeatedly", and the same is true for our trauma. If we do not deal with the hurt it caused us, trauma will still hold power over us. From that, we live out old, destructive patterns in our money. Our firefighter protector part finds numbing agents to avoid remembering and feeling the emotions. Pick your poison:

- Drugs/Alcohol

- Codependency/Dating

- Self-Harm

- Eating Disorders/Excessive Exercise

- Adrenaline Junky

- Retail Therapy/Shopping

- Workaholic

- Sex/Pornography

- Gambling

- Controlling/Micromanaging

- Scrolling Social Media

These are examples of how we can mask up and avoid dealing with our past hurts, wounds, and traumas. Feelings buried alive, stay alive.

Money manipulation or financial abuse are more common than one may think. It is when one controls another's ability to acquire, use, or maintain financial resources— lying about money, unexplained withdrawals, unpaid bills, shortages, blaming, using personal assets for individual gains—using money to control another person. One I have heard and seen, is a person taking money out of the account and stashing it away, without the other person knowing. Money secrecy can do damage in a current relationship and even future relationships. I have been in a relationship where my partner experienced this, and it is crazy how the lack of trust made its way into our own relationship. We carry our hurts, fears, and lack of confidence into our subsequent relationships if we do not do the inner work.

Let us talk about control. Do you know of someone in your circle that is in an unhealthy relationship, where one partner needs and has authority? Money can be held over someone's head: "I support you, so you have to do this." "You wouldn't have this life if it wasn't for me." "You're nothing without me." These are statements I have heard, and others have shared with me. Not everyone who has control over finances is good with money. I have seen it done where one's complete financial future has been dragged through the mud, and one's credit score ruined because of a partner. They have a hidden addiction that they are fueling. Be it gambling, porn, drugs, alcohol, or shopping, they are secretly living two lives. I am not sharing all of this to be a Negative Nancy. I want you to be educated and aware of the different signs when something does not seem right.

Is this talked about? Not when I was growing up. I see money manipulation often played out between divorced or separated households. I see this lived out between adults and kids; here is a fitting example: "but Dad gave me twenty dollars". Think about how the kids can play you, or using guilt or shame, you can use money as a tool. It is not about placing judgment or blame. This, my dear ones, is about awareness, acknowledgement, self-reflection, and choosing to live out our money differently. It takes one person to break a cycle. Let that person be you.

Once a lady came to me, as she struggled with holding a healthy boundary regarding money and her adult children. Her ex-husband was in an excellent financial position and would use money to gain access, acceptance, and control from their children. It worked. Suddenly, we, as moms, feel shame and guilt. We want to be able to offer the same things, regardless of our financial position, and we will do whatever it takes to remain in a good light. I have fallen into it, too. This was my advice to this sweet soul: Your future finances matter! Know the truth of what you can and cannot afford. It is okay to say to your children, young or old, that you are learning a different aspect of money and emotions. You recognize that because your feelings are high, that you may not make the best financial decision for your future. You need time to think this through, as you learn about your patterns and behaviors around money, and you need to have healthier boundaries from now on.

Share that this is a new perspective, and you are unpacking your money story. Be bold and say, "I have financial healing to do before I can commit to helping you with money, at this time. I love you and I am here to support you as best as possible, but I cannot do it financially."

Okay, now, all you moms who are reading this, did your heart break? It is hard to say no to our kids, and there are times when we it is necessary. Otherwise, we are hindering our own financial futures and enabling our own children. Ask yourself why you feel the need to help. Is it an emotion, and is the sentiment misplaced? I say misplaced because feelings of guilt and shame are often misplaced. Guilt is when you do something that goes against your core belief system. Having healthy boundaries never goes against your core belief system, so it settles misplaced feelings of guilt. Rebuke/reject them, reframe them, and move forward in the strength that you are taking power back.

Divorce is a traumatic financial event. Either side is messy and plays on our insecurities and fears. I know because I have lived through this life-shattering series of moments. Divorce can threaten our financial security and stability. With eighty per cent of marriages ending due to money issues, it is time as a society to start addressing what is really behind money: our emotions, wounds, and traumas.

Remember, we all have a money story based on what we were told, learned, and experienced. From that, we formulate our belief system. We bring our old hurts and wounds into new relationships and that breaks down communication. Our emotions then take over—when left to our own devices, we may lack rationale and wreak havoc on our money. I can recall now where I went from having a lucrative income in my house, to having little. I remember the sleepless nights, crying in the shower or a back alley. Praying to God, "What NOW, where are You now?" The pure desperation in my cries did not go away without leaving a mark. We are all marked by our experiences.

What are yours? They may be good or bad or even both. There is no right or wrong when it comes to our experiences; it is more just a matter of fact that this has happened and as a result, I have lived out my money in this way.

HEALING HURTS EXERCISE

Where do you carry hurt? Where does it come from? Can you look back and recognize that you were told something at an early age and have lived out your money story, good or bad, because of it? Did you grow up in a household where the man was in charge? Or a woman? Was there money manipulation or control? Can you reflect on where you might have learned behaviors throughout your lifetime? Reflection is key to making a change. What do you need to unlearn and relearn?

I will share a little story here, in hopes of shedding light on how, when we hear something repeatedly, we start to believe it is truth. No matter who tells us it is not, we look to find validation for it—the lie we believe. In my previous marriage, there were money superiority and identity issues. It is effortless to be an oil field worker and have your identity tied to how much you make. I have been told that making that kind of money is a blessing and a curse. "We can feel as though our only worth is in our wallet." Now I say these words, as these words were spoken to me. I know, deep in my heart, that no one's only worth is in their wallet and things can go south, and they sure did.

Our spoken words can be hurtful and wounding. Through this divorce, I was in a position where I needed to ask for financial help. It took every part of me to drop my damn pride and ego and do what was best for my/our kids and our future. Every bone in my body did not want to tell my ex that I needed his help, especially financial. Given I was the one that choose to leave the toxic marriage. I have carried the independent woman persona and asking for financial assistance was not an easy feat for me.

Prior to healing my mindset this ask would have been beneath me, and I would have rather suffered. Through my own healing I needed to be okay with asking and accepting help from others. When a man places all his value on what is in his wallet, this can become a story which is hard to break. Even though I am currently unaware of his financial healing journey, I hope he knows his worth is exponential, and not tied to his wallet. I share that with you as it is vital to be able to step back and look at the situation for what it is. His belief that his only worth was his wallet stems from a lifetime of spoken words, learned beliefs, and experiences that tainted his view of himself, others, and money. I, too, had a lifetime of thoughts that fueled my not needing anyone's help, as it was a sign of weakness. Breaking this down, so that I can still be an independent woman, with the help of others, has been freeing for me.

I will close with these words:

- We all have trauma.

- Everyone has attachment styles.

- We all have superiority complexes in different areas of our lives.

If you are reading this, and are thinking to yourself, "Hey, I do not!" You are operating from a fixed mindset. I hate to be the one to break it to you, but I am utterly shocked that you have chosen this book to read. Did I offend anyone? I call it how I see it, out of kindness and out of wanting others to change and be better. I am not here to be "nice." Nice would be saying what you want to hear, in hopes of getting something in return—not interested. I am here to better myself and you. You, my dear one, are not the only one that is doing this work. I, too, need to humble myself regularly, as I am not immune.

READER REFLECTIONS

Where do you even start with your reflections? Let us start by asking if you have ever experienced the following:

Money Trauma

- Financial PTSD from living at least three months when your income was not adequate to meet your expenses?

- Divorce/Separation?

- Money avoidance/denial or destructive money behaviors?

- Stagnant incomes, limited savings, excessive amounts of debt that cause crippling anxiety, worry, depression?

- Passed down generationally, relational, societal, or systemic money behaviors?

Money Manipulation
Have you ever encountered:

- Financial abuse involves controlling one's ability to acquire, use or maintain resources?

- Lying about money, making excuses, blaming, omitting financial details, and stashing away money?

- Unexplained withdrawals, unusual activity, unpaid bills, unexplained shortages?

- Ruined credit score from no fault of your own?

Money Infidelity
Do you have experience in any of the following:

- Spending in secrecy?

- Possessing credit cards, loans, and accounts, stashing away from partners?

- Incurring debt in secrecy?

- Unexplained spending/gifts/parcels?

Money Disorders
Are you prone to:

- Compulsive spending?

- Hoarding?

- Workaholism?

- Gambling?

- Financial Enabling?

Money Enmeshment
Have you been:

- Sharing inappropriate financial information with a child?

- Discussing ugly financial details after a divorce/ separation with a child?

- Using a child to avoid or deal with debt collectors?

- Oversharing information about money that is not age-appropriate or relevant to children or teens?

Now is the time to own one hundred per cent radical responsibility, with no judgment, as to what you have fallen into. What needs to shift and change so you can live out your finances differently?

I hope that this has prompted self-growth. Return to the lenses and dive deep into what is underneath them. What were you told, what did you learn, what have you experienced in your life that may contribute to your views on self and money. Remember, the more you put into this financial healing journey, the more you will benefit and create a ripple effect for your children/others.

Paying attention to your own money story is life-changing when you reflect and apply the work.

Chapter Twelve: Power in Our Money Stories

"Money is necessary, but not the determinant of a successful life. It is there to secure you but not to save you! It is there to support you, but not to sanctify you!"

–Israelmore Ayivor

Of course, we all have a story, and did you know we also have a money story? We will unpack how these two stories have played a significant role in how we live out our money. When meeting with people for the first time, I am a nerd about having money talks. People get weirded out by the excitement that bubbles out of me. I typically start out by asking non-typical questions. I am not asking you about your numbers; I want to know your memories. We are going deep, fast, lol. What was money like for you, growing up as a kid? When a gentleman asked me these questions, it caught me off guard, and I needed to put more thought into it. My parents did not talk about money; it was a hush-hush, taboo topic. I only recall them talking about it when money became an issue.

I have interviewed many people and asked these same questions. Everyone has a unique upbringing around money. Do you remember being on welfare and the shame that came with that? Some did. People recalled their parents always fighting about money, so they avoid the topic completely, as *they* don't want to fight. In contrast, others were given anything they needed and wanted. Do not worry. We will unpack this, too. I want you to put thought into what money was like for you as a child. What is your first memory of money? For me, it was when my parents lost a fair amount of money, and it changed the whole trajectory of our lives.

It may be buying yourself a lawnmower and going around to the neighbor's houses to make extra money to buy that sweet pair of Nike sneakers (you know, the high tops that were orange, with distinct-colored laces). The amount of detail about these first memories of money that others shared, was outstanding.

Another common one is parents helping you set up your lemonade stand or craft stand, and you taking your earnings to the store and indulging in a box of five-cent candies, not just a bag full, the whole box! Back in the day, when my parents would give my brother and I a dollar, we would take it to the store and ask for one-hundred one-cent candies, and then we would chuckle. We laughed because we got candy, and they had to count every single one, the good old days. We may have been shit-disturbers when we were younger!

I encourage you to ask your kids what their first memory of money is. My daughter shared with me, when she was sixteen, that her first memory of money was when we lost everything after her dad passed. Now *that* one is heavy. Some of us have heavy first memories of what money was like, and for others the memories are lighter. Either way, having these experiences shapes us and gives us what we refer to as part of our money story. The last chapter: money trauma, yes, you guessed it. It, too, forms part of our money story. Anything in life that we have been told, learned, experienced, and believed to be true, has a script or role in our money narratives.

I will go first and set the stage a little. We have subconscious beliefs, patterns, and lies about money. I can tell you stories about being bullied, single-family income, self-employment, corporate employment, being widowed, and being separated. In each event, I lived out money differently, based on my mistaken belief systems. I was not taught this stuff and certainly was not aware that events in life that have nothing to do with money, play a significant role in how we spend money. YIKES, that is right. Hence, why I am bringing this book: Rethink Your Financial Health to you.

Our money stories have power, and we must be aware of areas that can derail us on our journey. Sometimes it is unforeseen circumstances, and other times it is just being left to our own devices. It can be conscious and unconscious behavior patterns, which go unnoticed. When we dare to talk about money honestly; magic happens, financial wholeness is born, and my dear ones, this leads to financial freedom. We strengthen our relationships and our communication around money. Self-reflection and self-awareness create compassion for what others have lived, regarding their own stories.

Here are some words that come to mind when we think money: shame, guilt, fear, pride, anxiety, stoicism, numbing, entitlement, judgment, trauma, hustle, arrogance, striving, enabling, and manipulation—talking about money should not be taboo. We need to quiet the world's noise and break down and dismantle the old belief systems that no longer serve us well.

Your net worth does not define your value. Yet hear me on this: your net worth is the sum of all your financial decisions to date. Bankruptcy happens—unfortunately, when we are younger, we may be unaware of the magnitude of our choices. Lack of understanding about money, insufficient communication about it, and of course, the social pressure to keep up with our friend groups, all contribute. There is nothing worse than being in an excellent financial position and finally being able to move ahead but unfortunately, your previous, lousy, credit score, is holding you back.

Would you consider yourself naïve when it comes to money? Or do you have more of a "head in the sand" approach—meaning you do not look at money? In families, only one partner truly knows what is happening with the money. This is problematic, as all-hands-on-deck are required, when life throws us curveballs. We need to understand this. My family has repeatedly said that my dad would be lost without my mom. True story: who else comes from a family like that? This is something worth putting thought into; maybe it is the other way around for you, and your partner takes care of it all. What is your belief about who manages money in a home? Where does it stem from? Was it something you were told? Did you see it or learn it or did you experience it firsthand, in relationships of your own?

How often are you on the same page, with money, in a relationship? Opposites can attract. You may have one that is a saver through-and-through, and stability is their money language, while the other may be a person wanting to live in the now, have fun, spend money, and give experiences. So, how do we get on the same page, to reduce tension? First, we learn and understand one another's experiences with money and how and where our money stories took shape. Then, we work together to dismantle our misconceptions about finances. This one played out in my house, as I have said before, I will not ask you to walk something that I have not walked myself. My family is a prime example of money language opposites, as I am stable and, of course, he was the spender.

How many of us spoke these words: "I will not be like my parents, siblings, or friends?" You either use their lives as examples of what to do or not to do. One of my favorite sayings is: "More is caught than taught." Others are watching. So, how are you living out your money? Be sure to thank your older siblings if they have paved your way for the better. Sometimes, we watch others fall into poor financial decisions: addictions, gambling, and so much more, because that is all they know. We are creatures of habit, and we like it when we are comfortable. Change is uncomfortable.

My next point is, how was the environment you grew up in, regarding change? Did your family thrive in chaos or crumble under the pressure? When things don't go as planned, what was the first response? Fight, flight, freeze, and fawn are common nervous system responses. Be a detective and get curious as to where your responses stem from. What lens does your belief stem from? Is it true?

Here is one that I fall into; both men and women experience this one, and the main difference is language: men say, "Hold my beer!" while women flip the bird, saying, "Watch this." Both stem from hearing someone say we are not good enough or won't amount to anything. Have you felt unqualified? These experiences shape us, send us into striving and perfectionism, or an "I will show you." attitude. This is not always because someone has said these things to us; sometimes, we make up a story in our minds based on our feelings. Would you talk to your friends the way you speak to yourself? So often, we are our worst critics! The things we tell ourselves take root, too. Remember, what you give attention to will continually grow more prominent. What lies you are meditating on will take shape.

Others have shared some remarkable stories; I, too, have experienced this impacting our lives. I found this insightful: I have always told my kids that, "You are the sum of the five people you spend the most time with—choose wisely!" Another wise man mentioned that a community could have influence and impact your financial future. Are you part of a society where everyone is competing with "The Joneses," or is your community about gathering and belonging, a place where time well-spent is the currency. Remember, emotions drive our decisions in life. We want to belong and feel seen, known, and understood. When these emotions go unchecked, they take on their own agenda. We find other ways of being seen, known, and understood but sometimes in ways that are unhealthy and can lead to financial ruin. You have heard me say that emotionally connected people have better finances. This is because they have sharpened their skills at recognizing an emotion, understanding what is causing it, labeling it, expressing it, and regulating it. Take control and make wise decisions that are not numbing and deflective.

The stories were great to hear, mainly because they made me realize that men, too, struggle with numbing, retail therapy, or self-sabotage when it comes to finances. We laughed as we shared stories. Who can relate to having the best CD collection ever? Or buying video game console, after console? Taking trips or dinners that deflected what was going on in a marriage. Hell, I even shared that when I get a book in the mail, I quickly take it out of the box and put it on the shelf, so no one would ask. This whole book budget is challenging—the kids put me on a book budget as I have so many unread books. I then admitted this was money infidelity, and we laughed. Many of us do it but let us uncover *why* we do it. Whether it's a twenty-five-dollar book or a larger more substantial purchase, money secrecy is money secrecy. It breaks down our communication, erodes trust, and negatively affects our relationships.

Together, through awareness, we recognize our patterns of behavior. You can acknowledge when and where you have lived out your misconceptions about money. How have you contributed to where you are financially? Your stories, the lies we believe about money, become unconscious "money saboteurs." Defining emotions is enormous as it leads to dismantling the old patterns and lies. This breaks the power that our old stories have on us. Once we tear them down it is time to rebuild the foundation of our new story.

Other people in our lives have placed these labels on us, and we, too, have put our own labels on ourselves. These so-called labels are just stickers; you can peel them off— beautiful words from a sixteen-year-old! Let me repeat that, for those of you multi-tasking: labels others have placed on you are just stickers, they can peel off! I had a clever response: those stickers leave a residue—you bet they do, but did you know Goo Gone gets rid of that? It no longer becomes about others and what they think of you. Instead, it becomes more of who you want to be, who you are at your core.

Now, let us take it further and realize that our life experiences have led us to have a shape, a story about ourselves, that we believe to be true. I recently read the book, *The Art of Holding Space,* by Heather Plett. It shares a beautiful visual of how we outgrow our old stories. Now, I am amid my transformation, and between my two stories: my old story and my true story, the one where I am whole. I cannot help but wonder how true this is for so many of you reading. Creating a new foundation and a new narrative is key to living in the fullness of life and your money. Now, this space here, is scary—it is unknown. It means letting go of our old identities in life and money and allowing for space to explore this new you. It takes leaning into curiosity and possibility.

We have taken on our old stories as if they are our identity and we must stay there. I know who I am as I take a stand; I hold onto my old story, as it is all I know. Moving into your new story and rebuilding it will be uncomfortable; you will have insight, clarity, regret, panic, and peace. It is a paradox, in a way. The key is to show up and allow yourself to get to the other side of your story. Which is the actual transformation in your life, as it leads to you living out wholeness in your money. I have experienced this as tender and raw. It's messy, folks—just being honest, here! To shed the old stories that no longer serve us best, requires strengthening our intuition, our discernment, humility, courage, and curiosity. Bring your brave!

I love what Heather Plett says and here is why we end up lost within our own stories:

> We slowly but surely lose touch with our identity. We lose our free spirit, our uniqueness, and our authenticity. By careful imitation, punishment, and shaming, we learn how to survive the environment into which we were born. We take our wildness, our nonconformity, and our defiance. We put on masks to hide aspects of ourselves that we believe are unacceptable to the world. We become people our parents, teachers, and other influencers expect us to be. We learn to fit the culture.

Feel free to read that repeatedly—I did.

When this awakening happens, we realize that our old story is not who we are; it does not define us, and we face a new choice: to step into our own, unique expression. We can move away from insecurity of all kinds: the old labels we believed, disconnection, and lies. It is time to unmask and show up—even without having it all together. Please stop trying to impress others. It is time to tell the truth, reveal, trust, heal, and emerge into a transformational wholeness in yourself and your money.

Now let me share how trauma is a part of my money story. It has played a role in my finances ever since. It all started in Grades 7 and 8. We lived in a small town; my parents were entrepreneurs themselves and tried many things. One season they decided to buy an old house and fix it up. Their workmanship was terrific, and the home was beautiful. In grade school, it made us look as if we had money. I still remember having birthday parties at our house and getting the latest trends. I was one of the popular kids, and life was good. The time came when my parents got itchy hands, which in our home, signified moving time. I do the same thing and move lots—I always tell people it's because I don't like spring cleaning. So, sure, we sold the house and moved on to the next fixer upper. That is when things changed drastically for me. Next thing you know, kids were talking about us and the house we lived in. I received letters from classmates that I was worthless, utter garbage, and should do the world a favor and disappear. I ran to the bathroom to cry. I even made myself sick, so I did not have to go to school. I perceived that I did not fit in, that I did not have the right house, or clothes. You needed money to fit in with the popular kids.

Can you guess how I lived out my money from my teenage years to adulthood? I tried to fit in, bought the same things as other kids, so I would be accepted. I had to prove myself, prove that I was worth something, and material items were the way to do it. My first car was an old Volkswagen Golf GTI, and sure enough, the first thing I did was put a giant stereo system in it. Other kids in the parking lot would accept and include me. A couple of years went by, and I was like, "Oh yeah, watch this. You all said I would amount to nothing. Look, as I drive this new Mustang out of the showroom." I worked hard for my money and did it all by myself, and I wanted everyone to know it.

When I think back to that phrase, "Watch me.", I see that I did the same thing in my late thirties. My next significant memory of money was when my parents lost a tremendous amount of theirs. The stress that was on my parents caused an increased alcohol consumption, rocked my world. As I watched my parents build themselves up from the ground, it made me realize nothing in life is a sure thing. I began waiting for the other shoe to drop. As a result of this season in my life, I can reflect on the changes I made, to prepare for the future and save. I watched how hard it was for my father to ask one of his kids for help—it damn near broke him. The shame and embarrassment he felt were at his core; his eyes told me the story. I will never forget it, either. Guess who else has a tough time asking for help? I lived my life without asking for help, ashamed to look weak. If I had to ask for help, I felt I did not measure up enough. This experience drove me to please and strive, head down-ass up. If you want something done right, you must do it yourself.

Remember, we have filters on how we live out our money. What we were told and what we learned (I learned that asking for help was shameful, embarrassing, and that I did not want to do it). I experienced the ripple effects of what it meant for my parents to start over. Then I took all that and formulated my beliefs about money and life. It played out in all aspects of my life, both consciously and subconsciously. For years it was only subconscious, until I was challenged to view my life in the rear-view mirror. I realized if you do what you have always done, you will get what you have always gotten. I had patterns and behaviors that I needed to take one hundred per cent radical responsibility for and seek healing. That is the only way to live out differently.

Another memory I have is about work titles and status— of course, this shows up in our money stories. I was young and dating, bringing suitors to meet my parents. Now my parents are not shy about sharing their opinion; the apple does not fall far from the tree, there. I refer to this as "Constructive feedback with the best intentions". One of the gentlemen was older and was in line to take over his father's company. He was a mechanic who worked with his hands. He had a lovely, small house, and a reliable vehicle, so my parents were all over this one. On the other hand, I wanted another suitor's spontaneity, adventure, and wild spirit. He was younger, had a car but had no house, and jumped from job to job. Let us say, his future was not quite as promising to my parents. Being the rebellious teenager I was, I chose the adventuresome Bart, whom I married many years later and had three beautiful kids with. My parents' opinion of the young lad was no secret, as they clearly expressed it to us both.

I was told that these things mattered, that they were defining stuff in people—you could not change someone's drive or ambition. Now the beautiful thing was that I chose him; he was my diamond in the rough.

Here is where my perception is fascinating. Guess who I have held to that standard? Not others, myself. I let what I learned as a young teen take root deep within me. It stayed hidden for a while and did not rear its ugly head until I was widowed and trying to navigate being single. I was a kept woman. I took care of the kids, ensured the acreage was lovely, picked up material for the business, and did paperwork.

We had kids at an early age, and we dreamed that I would stay at home and raise them. We took any means possible to make that happen. I worked at a local bar for a season and ran a dayhome for six years to make ends meet, until the business took off. I was now attempting to enter the workforce, without education, or experience. Guess what, insecurities surfaced, and fast—my parents' voices were now in my mind. I had a challenging time silencing them. I was this nobody, without a bright future in front of me. I believed the lies my subconscious was telling me, and I say subconscious, as I did not know until recently what sent me into overdrive, striving, and proving. All those years back when I was made to feel like I did not belong, that I was the black sheep, the rebellious one—every family has one of those kids that others presume will be a bum on the street—I was that kid. I dropped out of high school, worked at a local factory, and did things the hard way. I married my high school sweetheart, had my babies, and moved far away.

Fast forward to 2015 it was time to show my worth to my family: I would get an education, a title, and an income to be proud of. I would climb that corporate ladder and show all of them—here, hold my beer!

Remember how I had said that my family voiced their opinions about my then-husband. Looking back with what I know now, he was driven by a sense of having to prove his worth to my family. "Watch this"—as we bought a house and vehicle; he even felt he had to upgrade my engagement ring to show them that he was making something of himself. He would always say to me, "I will get there, Hun, wait; by the time we are in our thirties, we will be set." He was a workaholic and always wanted something more. We got the house, and then it was another vehicle, then a boat, motorized toys, even Harleys. My husband's friends were welders in the oil field, bringing home the big bucks. Here is a big misconception that others and I have: oil field = big money. Well, it also comes with many other things too, which we won't touch on today.

The women in the local community assumed that my husband had oil field money, as he was gone and not at the kid's hockey, skating, or school events. Not at all the case, he was home every night. He had this goal: he was determined to be set by his thirtieth birthday. Then he promised me he would slow down and hire the staff to run the company. The "golden handcuffs" came into play— you want more when you make more, and you chase your tail to get it—lifestyle demands increase. Something I struggled with during this stage in our lives was that we were striving to prove that we were making it and in turn we lost our life.

I can look back now and realize that when I was a stay-at-home mom, I was a perfectionist. Homemade baby food, no chemicals, story time, craft time, you name it! My house was clean to the point that I was taking off stains from the trim along the flooring and the yard was always immaculate. Would I discipline the kids in public? Nope, I would wait until we got home. When someone new moved to the neighborhood, I would make a homemade meal and cookies to drop off. Would I leave the house with messy bun and sweatpants? Nope, I could never be seen like that in public. Would the kids not be put together to run errands? Not a chance. Gain weight in the winter? I would not risk it. I tried to live up to my idea of what a good mom, good wife, and good friend were. It burnt me out. I lived my life living up to others' standards, hell, the world's standards, or even the imaginary standards I placed upon myself. This would give me validation, that I had "done" it. I was somebody. I had value, meaning, and purpose. This season of my life was the biggest joke of all, now that I look back.

Let's talk about how I lived out my money: I was frugal, a saver, and balanced the chequebook. Ideally, if we needed something, we had it. I was so good at keeping our budget reined in that we were able to get ahead and start the company. By doing so, others would look in and think, "how you are you doing it? We make more than you and we are barely getting by." I would laugh, chuckle, and say we have no unhealthy habits. We did not eat out much, did not spend a whole lot, and neither of us had the terrible habits or toys that some other families had. We lived with one vehicle; I walked everywhere with the kids. Somewhere we got lost, as there was a longing to want what others had—the boat, the camper, and the vacations that became our reality. We, too, fell into wanting more. Part of this was our friend group and the community we lived in. Everyone else "has," so we must "have": the dirt bikes, the quads, the campers, the boats.

We longed for a simpler life, so we found a chunk of land and decided to build our dream home. She was a beauty, and acreage living played its toll on our marriage. There was so much to do, make, maintain, and prepare for. Every waking hour was occupied, and it took our joy— it was not what we thought it would be. Did you ever have an idea you thought was unique, and then once you accomplished it, it was different from what you expected? This, dear reader, happened to me, multiple times in life. As I am sure you can attest, as well. I mention these things as I want you to notice that throughout my life, events, people, and circumstances have contributed to my patterns and behavior with money.

Our emotions come into play and take the financial steering wheel. You will hear me say that friendships and neighborhoods can make or break your finances because I have experienced this firsthand. Here is a funny story: when we first moved to the area, we lived in a camper with three kids, a dog, and two cats. We used a friend's welder generator as we were without power. We hauled in water, and Bart used his plumbing skills to jimmy up a system that would allow our washing machine to work. The shop was priority before the house. Okay, so here we are, living the dream on this acreage, building our home. It is summer, so I am a low-maintenance woman at the time. We load up the kids, our shampoo, and head to the local water park to get cleaned up. I did not know anyone in the small town that we moved to, and here I showed up in my bikini, as that is just what I wore, and I thought nothing of it. What do you know—the park is quite busy, so we do not pull out our shampoo, but we get cleaned off. The kids were having fun as I ran in and out of the water. We headed back home and the next day I went into town in hopes of finding childcare for my youngest, who was two, so I could put sweat equity into the house-building process. I go to interview a lady in town and she yells out, "You're the new bikini lady at the park!" Oh, my goodness. I was not even sure how to answer that. "What am I?," I thought to myself. As it turns out, women in that town did *not* wear bikinis to the local splash park.

We were making waves within the community, building this shop, then a house. No one knew where we came from or who we were, as we kept to ourselves. Then, to top it all off, I show up "half-naked"—this is what the other women called it. I would get comments: "Must be nice to be an oilfield wife." I would look over, dazed, and pipe up, "My husband is not in the oil field. He is a plumber and gas fitter; we have our own company." That quickly shut them up, but I wondered what type of community I had moved into, that was judging us so quickly. I so desperately wanted to fit in, to be accepted. So, I tried to host scrapbooking parties, Epicure parties, and jewelry parties at the house, in hopes of getting to know the locals. Finally, they let me in, and life on the acreage improved. I became the talk of the town because I would run the country blocks and made healthy homemade snacks for the kid's functions. I was determined to be the mom that would make all the snacks for the holidays, and once my youngest was old enough, my goal was to volunteer at the school. I was a super mom—I liked this title. My pride and ego loved it when others would talk about my parenting, the kids' mannerisms, and my realistic eyeball cake-pops for Halloween.

I ended up lost in my title and lost who we were. I wanted the "best housewife" title. I kept up with my appearance, as I wanted my husband to be proud that he married me, out of all his choices. People pleasing was at my core, even when it came to money because it all stemmed from feelings of unacceptance and being a disappointment as a child. I did things the hard way. My poor parents—I was the rebellious one, the black sheep. I wanted to make them proud of me. I wanted them to see that I could do something right. I could be the best damn mother and wife because I was not the best daughter or student and did not have a career. So, this was my way of making it, of showing the world that I had value. By showing the world that Bart and I built a business, once again—here, hold my beer! He, too, had similar wounds. His parents did not believe in him—he was an outcast, did things the hard way, and dropped out of school in Grade 10. Together, we went against all the odds.

The collection just kept growing. Next thing you know, I remember sitting on the acreage we had built, and we were not happy. We could not understand it. We had come this far, and had everything, yet we were empty inside. Whispers circled, after he passed: "But he had it all, the wife, kids, house, acreage, successful business?" You know what he did not have? The feeling of enough. Of belonging, community, and hope. What he did not have was time. You will hear me say that time is currency, which is why it is worth far more than gold—you can never get it back when it is gone. How are you spending your time? Are you living and striving, thinking you will have a tomorrow? Heck, we all do, but there is a balance. Are you a workaholic and missing some of the most substantial years of your life?

I could go on for hours about this, as I believe that our lives, past, present, and future, paired with our emotions, have lasting implications, either good or bad, on our financial well-being. And I do not know about you, but hell, I want wholeness in my life, my money, and my relationships. Transcend your old story! I will end with two quotes, the first by John O'Donoghue, himself:

> Your soul knows the geography of your destiny. Your soul alone has the map of your future. Therefore, you can trust this indirect, oblique side of yourself. If you do, it will take you where you need to go, but more importantly, it will teach you a rhythm in your journey.

And of course, Brene Brown says, "You either walk inside your story and own it, or you stand outside your story and hustle for your worthiness."

ACCESSING YOUR MONEY STORY EXERCISE

The lenses of what you were told, what you learned, and experienced, helped you create a belief about your money story. Now, it is your turn to think about these lenses and your very own money story.

It may help to close your eyes, silence the world, yourself, others, and ask for these moments to surface. Leave room for whatever comes up. Your body will tell you to trust your inner knowing, to allow for healing in these areas. Take a deep breath and ask if there are more. When you feel you know, write them out, and work through them. Please do this as often as you need to. It is a process, uncovering the money story that is hindering your success:

Awareness: What keeps showing up in your money story? (Behaviors, patterns, etc.)

Acknowledgement: What is the story underneath what you were told, learned, or experienced? (It may not even be tied to money. It could be connected to your self-worth, identity, value, communication, bias, work, race, or anything.)

Self-Reflection: What is your ownership in your money story?

Defining Emotion: What emotions are in the driver's seat?

What's Under the Emotion: Are there other stories underneath or another emotion further down?

Dismantling: What is the lie you have believed because of the story you crafted and lived out?

Rewiring Truth: What is the truth?

Forgiveness and Healing: What is it costing you? Who are you harboring unforgiveness towards?

Living Out Your True Self: Give yourself compassion and grace. Repeat the truth of who you are in a mantra.

Reaching Your Financial Finish Lines: Build out a money roadmap.

When you can look at your lenses and see how your money story has been shaped through them, you must ask yourself: Now that I know this, am I going to change my behavior? Am I going to shift my perspective and live out differently?

I hope you answered yes!

To do this, you must have your head and heart on the same page. Your "head knowledge" needs to become "heart understanding." Only then can you live out your finances differently. If you only have head knowledge, you will have a blockage, and face resistance, every step.

It is time to break apart and dismantle the blockage that so many of us have between our heads and our hearts. It is easy to know something, and changing old beliefs is challenging work. You need to know, at the core of who you are, that you deserve abundance, freedom, and wealth, with no fear and no anxiety. You deserve overflowing opportunities for your financial future.

If there is even a slight hesitation as you read these out, go back and do more work on it. Why do you feel that financial change is not for you or your future? Is it a self-worth thing? An identity thing? Are the lives of others still holding you captive? Is it a lie you tell yourself?

I am here to tell you, that you are worthy of an abundant future, and it is yours to take. So, reach for it! Get good with being uncomfortable and push through the resistance that wants to keep you stuck. Be it, until you become it. Picture your wealth overflowing, building more opportunity for you and your family. You are fueled with purpose and passion for making the world a better place. Only you have the gifts that the world needs. So why are you robbing others of your talent? Why are you depriving yourself of a great future?

What is your head knowledge, as we are halfway through this book?

What are your thoughts that are rumbling around up there?

Is what you are thinking true?

What do you believe in your heart about finances and your future?

What do you believe to be true about your money story?

Can you shift your money story's narrative to one of abundance?

Once you have the Know and Believe figured out, what are your actionable items—small things you can do, that will move you forward?

What can you do to get one step closer to the future?

READER REFLECTIONS

Write out if anything is standing in your way.

What are your actionable items for the next thirty days?

Are there exercises you must go back to earlier in this book to dismantle or reframe a belief? You may have to reframe a belief repeatedly for a while. Remember, you have lived your life believing these lies so it will take time to overcome them. Keep at it; grit and perseverance will get you to the other side of this transformation to financial wholeness.

Chapter Thirteen:
Where in The Body

"Stress is caused by being 'here' but wanting to be 'there.'"

–Eckhart Tolle

Debt wreaks emotional havoc on our psyche. Financial strain affects all areas of our performance. Among the adverse effects of debt are low self-esteem and impaired cognitive functioning. You cannot learn, remember, be attentive, or solve problems while you are freaking out about money!

Money is a significant contributor to our health and wellness. Financial stress can mess with our sleep, our ability to think clearly, and cope with difficult emotional experiences. Financial stress can manifest itself in our bodies through physical symptoms such as anxiety, headaches/migraines, compromised immune systems, digestive issues, high blood pressure, muscle tension, heart arrhythmia, depression, and feeling overwhelmed. Shame and guilt can also show up throughout our bodies;

for me, it is in my shoulders and low back. You've heard me say it—our bodies keep the score! For me, it was crippling. My life experience had me in the fast lane, trying to numb everything I could, to avoid my feelings. As you can see in my story, not all our behaviors are tied to money, and yet every one of them affected my finances.

I have worked through my trauma and financial healing, which is why I am bringing you this chapter. For me, it showed up as inflammation, damage to healthy tissue, and increased risk for disease. It wreaked havoc on my digestive system, triggering my sympathetic nervous system (fight, flight, freeze or fawn). Prolonged flight or fight response led me down a path of undiagnosed illnesses. A hard season that I had to navigate without the emotional intelligence to recognize what was underlying. Financial healing is more than just your money; it is your overall well-being. This deserves your attention. Do you have symptoms in your body that are undiagnosed, or are you just chalking it up to getting older? The challenge of stress rears its ugly head in many ways. Where in your body are *you* feeling financial pressure?

Throughout this book, I may bounce around as I demonstrate/model where things can show up. I tell you stories so you can relate, as well as give you tangible tips, and tricks to help overcome your very own patterns and heal from your life. As I made this journey, I had to give myself grace, compassion, and understanding that I did the best I could, at the time. It will help if you do the same thing. Feelings will come up, good and bad. What is essential, is that when feelings surface, we work through them. It is time to take control of your life and push through resistance. Stop being stuck in the same place. Keep at it; this is not for the faint at heart. Dig deep, do the work of self-reflection, and you will find transformation.

Did you know that our emotions and life experience are stored in our minds and bodies? I did not know this until I discovered *somatic work*. Somatic is mind and body awareness. *Somatic therapy* integrates traditional psychotherapy, physical therapy, and holistic treatment principles. They use mind-body techniques to identify and release tension that affects our well-being. We can hold tension in our upper body. It feels tight, hurting our neck, shoulders, and upper back. Have you ever tried to relax those muscles? Of course, massage can help; you can use your lovely guns on yourself (ouch, ouch, ouch). Did you know there is another way to release tension in your shoulders? I will ask you to do this next exercise as I hope you will feel the difference, and it will drive my point home.

RELEASING TENSION EXERCISE

Sit on a chair, feet on the floor, back straight, hands dangling to the side of your body. Now raise your shoulders to your ears nice and slow (slow-slow) and give it one extra squeeze at the top and lower them back down as slowly as you can—the slower, the better, until they are back at the bottom. I want you to do these three more times and each time, see if you can melt/relax more than the last time. As you are doing it, where do you feel the release? What muscles are relaxing? Where is there still tightness? Is there warmth/coolness? Is there a numbing sensation? Take the time to journal what you feel, as you do this simple exercise.

When we are intentional about contracting our muscles and then releasing them exceptionally slow, we can relax those muscles more. It is a form of somatic movement contracting and tightening our muscles to trick our bodies into fully releasing. We often need to give our bodies the time or space to release. We are so tight that our emotions are locked in our bodies. When we are deliberate about contracting and releasing different body parts, our feelings may surface. We may even cry and not know why. That is okay; there is no right or wrong way to navigate this exercise. You may feel nothing or be overcome with sensations. Get curious about what is or is not showing up for you, as you do more of these exercises.

What is stored in the body affects our thoughts and feelings. They are inherently all connected. For example, our bodies hold stress and trauma. This could be trauma from a life-threatening experience, physical abuse, sexual assault, natural disaster, violence, racism or neglect. It could also be emotional trauma like bullying, emotional abuse or workplace trauma. Every one of us holds things differently within our minds and bodies. Regardless the source, all this trauma leads to health issues, including chronic, undiagnosed pain.

At a youthful age, I recall thinking I was doomed. That I would be crippled and unable to enjoy the life I wanted. So, I did internal work. I became a detective and learned about my body; all the emotions, hurts, wounds, and traumas I had swept under the rug for a long time. I could honestly say that I even disassociated from different life events, meaning I blocked them from my memory. I became disconnected from my experiences. Our bodies take over a form of protection and bring us into the sympathetic nervous system (fight or flight) in action, or the dorsal vagal, which is a system shutdown (fawn). As we work on ourselves, grow, and develop, we gain tools in our toolboxes that give us the ability to uncover and work through trauma, which brings freedom. You may be ready to bring things to the surface, or maybe not.

I strongly encourage you to get a counselor or therapist to help, if you have experienced any disassociation or trauma about things that surface. You do not need to work through this alone. Professionals are trained to help us bring up and release our trauma, big or small. Trauma has a place and requires your acknowledgment to work through it, so it no longer has power over you. When we disassociate as those memories surface, it is scary and feels surreal. Get the support you deserve for these instances.

I learned about the red light, green light, and centered body postures, which was a game changer for me. Here is a breakdown of each.

Green Light: A posture of outward force; if you refer to energy, it is outward moving. Blocked to receive, the chest may be forward, more of a dominant stance, head tilted higher than usual alludes to confidence, voice is substantively louder than most, talking *at* people versus talking *to* them. At first, people are drawn in and then repelled, as this posture is forceful, can be intimidating to others, does not listen well, and their way is often the only way.

Can you relate to this posture? I spent time at the green light, and here is why: I was striving and had a point to prove, that I could make something of myself. Here is a "hold my beer" approach, or "flipping the bird"— watch this, everyone! I was always the underdog, lacking education, experience, and others who believed in me. I strived for perfectionism. I was able to unpack that through my work. You, too, will be able to unpack the things holding you back from stepping into your true, authentic self.

Red Light: This is a posture of inward contraction, inward moving energy. Timid, with a lack of eye contact, blending in or going unnoticed, low energy and enthusiasm, and often viewed as weak or a victim. The shoulders tend to be rolled inward or hunched over, projecting feelings of isolation and invisibility. The head is down, posture withdrawn, non-confrontational and silent.

Is this your posture? Remember that this is just a guideline; you operate within all three postures, at various times. Reflecting on our posture and character traits allows us to have personal reflection and awareness and then transition to being truly you, without posturing.

Now, let us talk about the most authentic version of yourself and where we want to operate from regularly.

Centered: Your most authentic self is magical! This posture demonstrates inward and outward energy, both giving, and receiving. There is a sense of sovereignty and dignity with a relaxed, healthy carriage. The chin is level; this posture stands tall but is not forceful. Arms are relaxed, eye contact is easy, voice clear and natural. In this posture, you tend to magnetize people, are comfortable to be around, have a presence in the room, and are approachable and welcoming. Centered people build trust quickly and others are drawn in. They listen well, contribute with ease to conversations, value, and share space openly with others.

As you have identified, there is one posture you spend the most time in, which is normal. We are merely bringing awareness so we can shift and change our behaviors and recognize why we operate in these different states. Typically, our stories and lived experiences contribute to the condition or posture we spend the most time. Once we work through those stories and release them in our bodies, we can live out a new narrative. One that is genuinely YOU and unique as a fingerprint. Ask yourself where you see yourself. What is your default posture: green or red or centered?

My default shape is a green light, sometimes red, but seldom. I did everything the hard way; I forced my way in the world and when it comes to confrontation within my home dynamics, I can shift between the two. My ex-husband was exceptionally good at getting me out of centered and back into my green and even red, at times. I believed the lie that if you want something done right, you must do it yourself, that others will let me down, or not have my back (this is an old abandonment wound). Asking for help for myself, I believed, was a sign of weakness. If I asked for help, I would be viewed as unqualified. I sometimes feel back pain when I operate in a green posture.

Can you recognize when and how you might live this out? What are you telling yourself because of this? What are the lies that you believed? What does it cost you, to operate in *your* dominant pattern? Be specific.

I hope that by going first, I am helping you to reflect and journal your own process. Not having any support caused me feelings of isolation. It caused me burnout, as I did not let anyone in to help me. Me, faking it till I made it left me not being true to myself. I wore a mask pretending my life was good. I did this for a long time.

Given your understanding of green, red and centered lights did something new come up for you, or is the old narrative showing its ugly head again? Release it, let it go, and work through it.

There is an ebb and flow of life that leads us to make the choices we do. I hope you can find similarities to your own life and that my story and my journey can help you. Once we know how we have lived out our money due to the lenses of what we were told, learned, and experienced, we can make changes and adjust. We can recognize the emotions easier, which allows us to make better financial decisions. When we efficiently self-regulate our emotions, the easier it is to reach our financial finish lines. We must dismantle our old money stories that have contributed to subconsciously sabotaging our futures.

Doing the inner work allows for a complete life-shift. Wealth begins within; financial healing and letting go of our shame, guilt, and embarrassment is the starting point. Before we can even start, we need to be aware of where and what we are feeling. Healing our old wounds allows us to release the old patterns and live our true abundance. Part of this work is getting back to the *you,* that you were designed to be, all along. Let's be real though, life happens. We take shapes that others impose on us, or we become something else, in hopes of pleasing others. We chisel away at our beliefs about ourselves, our families and our money. I realized that my actions, and my words had a ripple effect. It gave others a perception that I was demanding, overpowering, too much, hard to manage, intense. That list could continue awhile.

Here is a quick summary of the three lights of somatic body postures.

Red Light: Inward posture.

- Timid, lacks eye contact.

- Often ignored, unnoticed, overlooked.

- Avoids arguments and confrontations and gets walked over by others.

Green Light: Forceful posture.

- Chest forward.

- Dominant stance - hands on hip, here I am.

- Comes across as aggressive and domineering.

Centered: Aligned, balanced and aware.

- Relaxed, healthy posture.

- Magnetizes people – fully present.

- Self-awareness.

In our lives, we tend to operate in one posture predominantly and, given certain circumstances, can move into another. However, when we go deeper as to where we are storing these wounds within our bodies, we start to notice that it can also be a contributing factor if we operate in the green or red light. Our goal is to continuously live from our most authentic self, which is centered. This is also known as the ventral vagal system of connection to self and others. We must practice because we have a history of operating in the other two.

To illustrate this point, let me explain the wounds from men I experienced. This has played out in my finances and multiple relationships, without consciously knowing it, until recently. After my world shattered, I vowed never to trust another man or give another man that kind of power. When I say authority, I mean jumping two feet in, trusting with all aspects of my mind, soul, body, finances, future, dreams, and goals. Going to the opposite extreme like this is not healthy either. However, I did what I had to do during that season. Do I hold shame, guilt, or embarrassment? I did, until I was able to recognize my ownership and give myself the grace and compassion that I did the best I could with what knowledge I had at the time. That is precisely why I love my tagline, "Sharing the manual." I did all this, so you could learn from my mistakes, which I am highlighting here in this manual. Oh, my goodness, too funny!

I remember others who knew and loved Bart, looking at me and saying, "Amie, we lost him, too." This would send my mind and body into a complete downward spiral: Hell no, Bart was the father to *my* kids, *my* husband, counselor, lover, friend, confidant, financial provider, and protector. Bart was my *everything*.

Now, our circumstances may be different than what others experience when they are starting over, but for me: I did not have my own account or credit score! Yes, I managed the money and all the bills got paid, but my husband was our home's primary source of income, which ended abruptly when he passed. You've heard this story earlier, so I won't go deep into it. This meant getting rid of everything, moving to a new location, getting rid of our animals, and driving away with our acreage in the rear-view mirror. The only life I knew, now in boxes in a semi-trailer. This sent me to the green light, going one hundred miles an hour. When I say fast track, oh hell yeah, I tried to fast-track that chapter. Even worse, I tried to numb myself using all types of behaviors—drinking, dating, eating, spending money, scrolling aimlessly on social media, sex, and exercise.

When one thing stopped working for me, I moved to the next, hoping to get by, and suppress my feelings. I became the serotonin, oxytocin, and adrenaline junkie. I kept my addictions quiet, which is easy when society deems them okay. All my numbing behaviors were viewed as acceptable, and they were tearing me apart. They used up all my savings, took away my identity, and left me feeling worthless, unvalued, outcast, exiled, unaccepted, and unforgivable. You can imagine how life responded to me when I viewed myself this way. I was incredibly good at wearing a mask. As I said, I mastered the green light, and when no one was looking, I would fall apart in the back alley in my vehicle, now in the red light and playing the victim.

BODY POSTURE EXERCISE

Now, ask yourself what body posture (red light, green light, or centered) do you wish to operate from, and why?

Looking back to what you were told, learned, and experienced, can you see where you picked up different beliefs that led to you operating in a green or red light?

Unpack the lenses that you have taken on throughout life:

What is it costing you?

What would this new shape look like? How would you live out? Get detailed.

Stay curious – what gifts and qualities have you not shared with the world?

What could be possible if you expressed them? Close your eyes and imagine. It may seem strange at first but give yourself time. Not expecting anything; just letting things surface.

Let us shift to possibility now. What is the truth about you?

What is inside of you that you wish to share with the world? Be specific again.

What do you deeply desire?

What do you deeply need?

I needed acceptance, belonging, safety, stability, creativity, curiosity, adventure, trust, authenticity, fun, humor, movement, rest, inclusion, compassion, peace, joy, love, and spontaneity. An extensive list, I know, and it is time we set our intentions. Go big or go home.

Know: Head knowledge.

Believe: Heart understanding.

Do: Planning action for a different outcome.

What will it feel like if you can achieve this?

How can you gain traction, release your old story, and operate in the center of your most authentic version of yourself?

Stand in the future and picture yourself and where you are - describe it in detail. How does that feel in your body?

Use your five senses, close your eyes, and envision the future. What do you feel, touch, taste, smell, and temperature, and what are your surroundings like?

In doing this exercise you're connecting your head and your heart. By now you get to think this abundant life, this wholeness, is for me, and I will have it.

Write out your beliefs about your future and how you will get there.

READER REFLECTIONS

Is there anything in this chapter that has surprised you? What stood out? You may want to learn more.

What areas do you wish to research to enhance your learning and understanding?

Remember to "Be it until you become it." Believe in your heart that you have hope and a prosperous and lavish future.

Chapter Fourteen:
Money Languages

"Money speaks only one language: If you save me today, I will save you tomorrow."

–Unknown

Let us dive into the different money languages. You may have heard of Gary Chapman's five love languages. Understanding others' love languages allows for us to have better relationships. We can recognize what we need, along with what others need from us, to feel loved, appreciated, and belong. We also have money languages. Over the years, I have learned about different wealth languages from Cale Dowell, and I will summarize them for you. (Going forward, I refer to them as money languages versus wealth languages.) Knowing your own money language, as well as your partner's, and your children's' money language, is essential. This helps to enhance all your communications regarding money. Our money language often stems from our money stories and the lenses through which we have lived life: what we were told, learned, experienced, and believed to be true.

Let us go through the four money languages—you may fall into one of them. You may also demonstrate traits in others. What is essential to take away from this is that every money language has pros and cons. Understanding how you fall into the money language spectrum is vital information, as it will allow you to have better compassion and empathy for others' past financial decisions. It will also give insight into how you can set yourself up to make wise financial decisions, in the future.

Stability: This is me, to a "T"! The glue that holds it all together. That is right; you are the big guns—a next-level nurturer. You value money and you have a keen sense of creating security for yourself and those you love. You open your heart and home to give others a stable environment. At your worst, you can be paralyzed by unrealistic fears. I get you. We go out of our way and can get lost in the weeds trying to deliver on "stability." Sometimes we are referred to as the classic worrier—I prefer attentiveness! Consider building up your future need for an emergency fund, hammering down on the mortgage, retirement planning, holidays.

Common traits:

- Focused on near term.

- Typically risk-averse.

- Keen sense of creating financial security for self and others.

- Does not enjoy talking numbers but wants to know everything.

- Ensures money is available for bills, repairs, kids.

- Can be paralyzed by an unrealistic fear of delivering stability.

- Unwilling to discuss finances.

Future: Did you guess this to be you or your partner? Of course, you did. Predictable, making sense of it all. You've got it going on! Checklists are your superpower; you could talk numbers for hours. Analytics—yes, please! You want all the details and more. You have a roadmap in your back pocket, as well as plans B and C. Keep in mind that at your worst, you are susceptible to paralysis. At your best, you bring consistency and balance to relationships. You help friends and family navigate their finances, as you demonstrate great patience. This is no surprise to you, but you are not keen on significant risks. Your focus is on preparing for tomorrow and all the potential detours life can throw at you. Your main objective is to answer the following questions:

How much is enough? Where is my finish line? Am I protected? Did I communicate the plan with my partner?

Common traits:

- Focused on future.

- More risk-averse than opportunity or moment peeps.

- Use money to reach future goals: retirement, college.

- Often analytical, enjoys talking numbers.

- Brings financial consistency to relationships, disciplined, thorough decision-making skills.

- Does not manage curveballs well, cannot see beyond own plan.

- Typically, future people have plans that may be unknown to their partner.

Moments: Beaming with JOY, the life of the party. Others are drawn in by your flair, but you knew it all along—you are unforgettable. As others describe, you can be a whirlwind, in a beautiful way. You bring fun and laughter to any room. You view money as a way of having memorable moments with others, which has tremendous value. But, at your worst, too much fun without considering the math, can ruin your future finances. You are uniquely equipped to put money to use for the most enjoyment in life. When paired with others in one's life, there are moments it can get rocky. I will say it like it is here – a "moment" person has the highest emotional risk of falling into irresponsible financial decisions. If it feels good, you are in! Forgive me for reminding you that the moment itself does not always require money. It requires ONLY YOU! You bring the goods, the fun, and the laughter. *You* are the experience!

Common traits:

- Focus on near term.

- Motivated by memories and experiences.

- Typically help others enjoy life, generous with assets.

- Utilize money for the enjoyment of life.

- Can fall into a "keeping up with the Joneses" mentality.

- Irresponsible or self-serving financial decisions.

- Can be quickly taken advantage of.

Opportunity: You know this is you or you can spot your partner—shocker! You dreamer, you. I am not going to lie; you are a force to be reckoned with. When it comes to thinking ahead, you have it going on. You are a visionary. Intrinsically, you understand the concept of risk versus reward. Fear does not stop you; you view money to build and capitalize on what you see as an opportunity. You have an unclouded vision for money and its deployment. At your worst, a sense of reason may leave your thoughts, putting you at risk. You do not sweat the small stuff; it's go big or go home! Am I right? When paired with other dreamers, you tend to "act" with feelings, rather than details. You trust your gut. Have you thought much about this opportunity's purpose? Is it creating unnecessary risk? Who can you have on your team that gets to the smaller details, ensuring a return on investment? Put some thought into this.

Common traits:

- Visionaries, with a clear picture, and a purpose of wealth.

- Well thought out strategies, efficient at decision making.

- Focused on the long term, willing to take risks.

- Motivated by future dividends.

- Money is a tool to create more advancement.

- Not too fond of small numbers—these are big picture peeps.

- Act on feelings rather than details—trust your gut approach.

Now, with anything, you do not fit into a box, nor do I want you to. These are just guidelines to reference and discussion points to help you get to know yourself and your partner, better. You may find yourself between two "money languages," depending on the season of life you are in. What is most important is to understand the money story underneath and openly communicate what you are feeling with one another. Know your weaknesses and be aware when you are falling into them. Talk openly about your feelings and what is underneath them. I love an exercise from one of Brene Brown's books:

IS IT TRUE EXERCISE

This is the story that I am telling myself based on what I know. Is this true?

Can you please reframe it with the truth of what you are trying to say or do?

You then need grace to accept truth, in order to cancel the story that you have made up in your head. Self-reflection, my beautiful peeps. Of course, we are circling back to the lenses through which we manage money from: what we were told, what we learned, and what we experienced, and what has formulated our belief system. When you look at the different money languages and profile yourself into one of the four categories, take it even further and ask yourself:

What were you told throughout your life that would have you believing and falling into this money language?

What did you learn that contributed to your patterns and behaviors with money?

Experience only helps to solidify what you have already been told and learned, and this is the one that has weight. So, what happened in your life to bring about these traits in this money language?

You can use the four lenses in all aspects of your life! Being a money coach, I put most of my focus on that, but these tips, tricks, and exercises will work in all realms of your life.

Know: head knowledge.

Believe: heart understanding.

Do: when both are in alignment you can live out differently.

Now break it down to what is the truth about what you know.

Is it the truth?

Deep down, do you believe it to be true?

What would your future self say to this belief of yours?

What is the truth?

And, of course, with the truth, what is possible for you to live out?

That is the do; now write it down.

What actionable items can you do within the next 30 days to become the future you?

Head knowledge becomes heart knowledge giving you the momentum to live it out. Words without actions are dead people.

READER REFLECTIONS

Take the time to share these money languages with your partner and children. Ask them what category they think they would fall under. Do not rush over to them and say, "Hey, did you know you are a moment person? I just profiled you." STOP, let them determine what they think they are and explain their reasoning. Be open, curious, and lean into what may be possible if you are to openly discuss what money was like for them as a kid: their first memories of money and the different lenses through which they do money. Start small. Go in with no expectations, just the desire to learn more about your loved ones.

What have you learned from this exercise?

Did anything surprise you?

How did your partner receive this information?

Did you share it? If not, why? What is stopping you?

Is resistance showing up? What could be under it?

Chapter Fifteen: Masculine & Feminine Energy

"Money is energy. It reflects how we treat ourselves."

–Rachel Peavy

Communication is more than just talking; it is about connecting. Most communication is not done through words but rather through body language, tone of voice, behaviors, actions, and energy. It is the energy between people that brings us to the fascinating topic of masculine and feminine energy, which plays out in our money.

Regardless of gender, we all contain both masculine and feminine energies. Our leading energy reflects the core of who we are and our values. When we understand our primary energy and are aligned, we live out profoundly. When we are not aligned, we are simply chasing anything and everything in hopes of feeling fulfilled and happy. It begins within us, to discover, lean into, and embrace our primary energy. This will help us discover our tendencies within relationships and understand how we behave. It is essential to clarify that you can be a woman with masculine energy and be aligned, or you can be a man and have feminine energy at your core. We are all individuals and find alignment with either of these energies; there is no right or wrong.

Let us break down the energies:

Feminine Energy: awareness, seeing and feeling everything, connection, both parts of the brain are active simultaneously, taking on everything at once, multi-tasker. Feminine energy is about "being." It is nurturing, intuitive, cherished, honored, and embodies desires being pursued. If you can resonate with this within your core being, when living from this place, you will find alignment.

Masculine Energy: focused on one task at a time, total concentration, solution-driven, fixing, analytical, impatient, assertive, and logical. A "masculine" is a "doer." The hunter pursues a chase, loves a challenge, and wants to be needed. You may see yourself here, or you may go between them both, which is normal. However, we all have one that resonates more. In different scenarios, we will shift between the two energies—be sure to remember and pay attention to when and why you have shifted.

The best way to achieve greatness in all aspects of your life and your money is to be in a complementary relationship. What changes a relationship from good to great is the spark that is between us. Having commonalities is good but may not produce that spark that takes it to a great level. Note-I am not talking about a sexual spark, although it may be enhanced.

Likewise, having a partner with the same energy is good but could be better. To maximize and play to the masculine and feminine energies, you need to determine your primary energy and live aligned with it, so you attract the opposite energy. It does not mean that you do not have the same core values as your partner; you may see that in an energy that complements your core.

There are some things to remember and be aware of. Primarily, these are things that affect our core energy, such as stress or exhaustion. Close to burnout, people will start to operate in the opposite energy and that causes disconnection. Disconnection is a form of protection: masking up, controlling, and taking matters into one's own hands, which cuts off all energy. When we shift, we want to be aware of it, to take inventory and reposition ourselves. This may mean we open communication and ask for help. It may sound like this: "I find my energy shifting; this just happened. I think this may be under it: _____. I would like your help before we both shift out of alignment, creating disconnection." This only works if you understand your core energy and have the emotional intelligence to work through feelings and find the root cause. One of the parties may need more guidance and patience to initiate this conversation.

I have said that when one leads others to follow, the domino effect occurs. Set this footing as your foundation, and you will see others learn these behaviors. Before long, everyone's emotional intelligence will increase. Think of your home thermostat setting the temperature—you can be that thermostat.

When a person's feminine energy is squashed, they will mask up with masculine energy. They will seek the feeling of being seen, known, and understood elsewhere, to access that feminine energy again. Here is what kills feminine energy:

- When one feels unsafe.

- Not being seen, known, or understood.

- Lack of empathy and compassion for what the person is going through.

The same is true for the masculine energy: when killed, they will mask with feminine energy. Meaning the partner will not feel protected, safe, or pursued.

Here is a list of things that kill masculine energy:

- Criticism.

- Controlling and micromanaging.

- Being closed off.

Our energies play an essential role in our intimate relationships, parenting, and finances. We talked earlier about red light/green light postures and how our bodies can take the toll of it, when we are out of alignment. Given that feminine and masculine energies are at the core of who we are when we are not in alignment, they have lasting effects on our partnerships, choices, and behaviors.

I share this with you as I look back at my past relationships and recognize when I had switched to masculine energy and masked up. As a result, I was not feeling seen, known, or understood, which killed all passion, connection, and trust. This led to other problems within our marriage. I recall being told I was emasculating my partner. Now I get it: it was because my feminine energy was gone. I was operating in a managing, controlling, and get-it-done mentality that sent my partner into the feminine energy. That get-it-done mentality is when our nervous system works in the sympathetic, fight-or-flight response. Reflecting on this allows us to regulate and reposition, so we are more aligned with our primary energy. This can be a game changer, folks.

Remember that masculine energy can be a superpower. One you may need to tap into at times to make things happen and to assert your confidence. Do not stay there if it is not your core alignment.

Guess what happens if you have feminine energy at your core and you kill the masculine energy in your partner, or your own energy gets squashed? You find that your partner is no longer attractive because they are no longer your protector and are no longer pursuing you from that masculine energy. Instead, they may seek you from the feminine energy, which may be seen as needy and undesirable. If this has been your pattern, have no fear. That is why I brought it up as this was also my pattern. When we know better, we can do better. The beautiful thing with all of this, is that we are unlearning and relearning how to make better partners, parents, community members, and all-around good humans, while kicking ass in our finances!

No masculine energy wants to be told what to do. The reason this is important to understand is because it plays into our money. We are only human; we all get out of alignment. We are more vulnerable to fall prey to numbing behaviors, emotions, and/or insecurities. This could include drinking, pornography, retail therapy, gambling, or drugs—pick your poison. Numbing behaviours often come at an expense to the pocketbook. When out of alignment, we look to other things to feel good, and our emotions, if left unchecked, can hijack our financial future.

So, how do we stay in alignment? First, we need to go back to our energy lens and see whether we are living out the most authentic version of ourselves or are we living out what other people have told us? Are we being what others say we should be? Are we behaving in a way that does not fuel us but instead makes others happy?

People-pleasing perfectionism can cause us to live in an energy that is not our authentic design. Time to check in.

ENERGY CHECK-IN EXERCISE

What were you told about masculine and feminine energies?

Were you told that females are feminine, and males are masculine?

(This is not always the case.)

What have you learned about energy types?

Think back to your senses: what did you hear, see, smell, touch, or taste, which has given you misconceptions about your energy?

Can you look back to an experience where your masculine or feminine energy was squashed, and you didn't know it?

Have you believed you were the opposite energy when you felt more aligned with the other?

What we need to remember when we learn about energies, is recognizing what makes us feel alive. It is not about what others think, say, or do. We do not fit into a box; we are all unique and have different attributes. For example, you may be a woman with masculine energy or a man with feminine energy. Suppose you identify as they/them, you need to find which energy feels right with your inner knowing. It can be any variation; remember, it's your core. It is where and when things fall into place more easily. Abundance can only happen when you live in proper alignment. We are in a time where we're shifting our perspectives on what our future looks like. We are embracing lives of abundance, fulfillment, happiness, wealth, health, and prosperity.

To do this, you must shed all the labels others have put on you. You must get back to the core of who you are and what you want in your future. Deep down, we all have an inner knowing and it is waiting for us to trust it, so we can live out our true purpose. We have spent our lives not listening to our inner knowing, while the noise of our families, friends, society, and social media, took over. It is time to strip down. Metaphorically—my peeps, do not get naked on me while reading this book...unless that's your thing, in which case, strip away, but I don't need to know.

Below is the Know, Believe, Do model-a life raft, which will take you out of sinking water and save your life, if you let it. Remember, the choice is yours.

Know: head knowledge.

Believe: heart understanding.

Do: ability to live out truth.

What do you know to be true?
What if something else was true?
What would be possible if you lived aligned?
Do you believe in your heart that you deserve to live aligned?

I hope you do. If you hesitate, that is okay, too. Then, we need to go back and work on what lies you still believe about your future.

What is standing in the way for you?

How can you live out with this newfound knowledge about yourself?

What are your next steps to living differently knowing what you now know?

READER REFLECTIONS

Now it's your turn to reflect on these questions—develop a game plan for your future and how you will take back the steering wheel. Remember this is not a place to judge yourself. Instead, you are giving yourself self-love and compassion. You did the best you could in the season you were in. The choice is yours as to whether you will stay there. Choose your season; choose your hard:

Being single is hard and being married is hard—
choose your hard.
Being skinny is hard, being bigger is hard—
choose your hard.
Being rich is hard, being poor is hard—
choose your hard.

Change your perspective on the future; shift and be who you want to become.

You are in there, waiting to be free—you are the only one holding yourself back.

If you want freedom from your past, freedom from fear, anxiety, worry, and freedom from a scarcity mindset, then step out and do things differently. It starts with one hundred per cent, radical responsibility as to how you have lived out and recognizing why you have lived this way, all through a lens of curiosity. Always go back to the four lenses when you are doing your reflection: what you were told, learned, experienced, and believed to be accurate. Then, think to how these are serving you-and your future.

Chapter Sixteen: Dismantling

"Demolition is a part of construction."

–Daniel Wilson

Do you already feel as if the foundation under you is in pieces? That we have cracked you open and exposed all those parts of you that you have worked hard to hide? I know that I sure did and still do, at times. I am so immensely proud of you for coming this far; you are courageous and brave! Remain curious and trust the process of why and how it all works, to integrate you into your most authentic self.

Mindfulness is the art of what we are all doing to reach wholeness. It is not about banishing thoughts or feelings. It is about noticing, labelling, being curious, and letting feelings pass through you, without becoming attached. It is a "flow-through" approach. This is key, as we all have what I refer to as "triggers" or "activators": things that cause our emotions to take over, elevate our heart rates, increase discomfort, and so forth. We need to recognize when emotions surface: dismantle them and replace them with the truth. When a thought comes, please do not send it away. Work through it, wrestle it to the ground, and find the underlying cause. If you try to shame it, banish it, or hide it, it will take greater hold of your mind. What you think about, grows.

Be sure to spend time journaling about what your triggers have been and what may still be. So much of our upbringing has been hardwired and indoctrinated us and our programming has malfunctioned. We all have stories, trauma, and wounds that need healing. This will help us to fully rewire and change our patterns and behaviors in our life and our money. If you have been doing the exercises—great, as that is rewriting your pathways each time. If you are not, no worries, you can always go back and start—better late than never. If you want change, this is how it starts: doing the little things that become the important things. This is how you gain traction and momentum.

I am a reader, and some books kick my ass: I fall flat on my face, shatter to the floor—cracked open, exposed, naked metaphorically, and alone to pick up my pieces. It was once said to me that potters use previously broken pottery, as it strengthens the new clay. That is beautiful, and I now have a love for pottery, as it lives multiple lives. It is made new, once broken, and reshaped, to be even better than before. Newsflash, my friend: you are pottery and each time that you feel as though you are broken and shattered in pieces, you will be made new, into something more beautiful. Sometimes we need to be broken, to be molded into our true design.

It may seem as if doors keep closing on you and you are always waiting for the next door or even a window, to open. Got to love that old saying: "when one door closes another opens." How come no one tells you that, at times, you are waiting in the hallway, and the hallway sucks? Let's be honest—we have all had seasons that were hard or *are* hard, right now. Ask yourself, is life happening to you or is it responding to you? What do you believe about yourself and your life, that is holding you back?

This dismantling phase is not a pretty one. When I was going through it myself, I felt very alone, as if no one understood what was happening. The best way for me to explain it to the ones closest to me, was that I was between two stories: the old me and the real me. The future me I so badly wanted to live in, and the old me was extremely comfortable and would feed me lies, to keep me stuck. It felt as though I was in a tug-of-war between those two versions of myself. I knew this old me, inside and out; she had attributes that I liked and others that were not so great. This future me was unknown. I would get images, feelings, senses, and a longing for what my future held, and the unknown caused resistance. When we face resistance, it is important to talk about holding space. I say this, because holding space for someone you are close to, when they are in this unfamiliar place, can be hard—especially when you have skin in the game. When we have skin in the game, we can try to fix things, or take over the journey—hijack is a word I would use often, with family and friends: "Please do not hijack my healing journey. I need to go through this, feel it, process it, work through it, and get to the other side." I will be transparent here. Not everyone in your circle can hold space in a healthy way, for you. Find your safe people.

Whenever we grow and become better versions of ourselves, we will have some naysayers that do not like or want this change, as it is unfamiliar. This has nothing to do with you: it has to do with their own hurts and the lenses through which they experienced life but have not worked through yet. You need to stay the course for your own healing and wholeness. You will have people fall out of your life and new ones come in. It may be for a season, and it may be longer. We all have our own journeys, and we need to be supportive for ourselves and others—to become the best versions of ourselves and live out our true alignment.

Will it be lonely? It may, and it may not. You may find yourself building up new friendships and expanding a whole new way, as you are open, curious, learning, and growing. Whenever we are open to learning and growing, we are magnets and the right people come our way. We are not meant for everyone; the sad truth is that it took me forty years, to figure that out. A wise man said to me, "Amie, think of yourself as a magnet. You will attract those that are drawn to your passion and energy, and you will repel others." Mic drop! I had to learn to just "BE". The right people will be magnetized and guess what? It is true. I tell you this, as I want you to be hopeful. As you shift and change your future, you will experience discomfort. Pushing through the resistance is what leads and propels you forward to an amazing future that is aligned with the core of who you are and the role you play in this world.

The important thing to remember, is that our behaviors and patterns with money do not always stem from what we were told, learned, or experienced, regarding money. Our behaviors and patterns develop around our self-worth, our identity, and so forth. This is where the lenses come into play, and we need to break apart our lives in every realm to uncover areas that play into our money. This requires intention, grit, and perseverance, as we look to build new neurological pathways. It can be like an old, muddy, dirt road, with ruts that can suck you back. Stand tall, know your truth, and always bring your best self forward. At times, we can stumble and fall. It happens. What is more important at this moment, is what you do after you fail.

Part of the work in dismantling is that we need to recognize, reflect, rebuke, and reframe to reposition. To replace an existing belief, you need something to replace it, allowing you to reposition yourself, to move forward differently.

When we look at our lenses, we can determine that something is off. Right then, we need to work through the Five R's:

Recognize: Where it is coming from, what is under it, and how is it playing out in my life? Is it hindering my success or leveraging it?

Reflection: What is underneath the emotion, the lie, the root problem? How is it serving me?

Rebuke: the lie. Once I determine that it is a hindrance, I need to rebuke it—not take it on as my truth.

Reframing: This means turning it into an empowering statement, a truthful statement that will shift and change perspective. (This is often where we need to speak out our truth, have a mantra, or sticky notes, to remind us of our truth.)

Repositioning: Is possible when I reframe with empowerment. I can move forward and live differently with the newfound truth.

Do this in all areas when it comes to your money. I encourage you to create money affirmations, and money mantras. Here are some examples:

- *I am worthy of prosperity.*

- *I am enough, I create abundance, I generate growth, I am a money magnet, and I have no limits.*

- *My future is bright.*

What we hear, think, and speak, plays a role in our lives. What you put out there, finds its way to you. Words have the power to build up or destroy. Are the words you are speaking building up others, as well as yourself, or are they tearing down? It is easy to talk nice and be kind to others. Now, are we offering that same gentleness, kindness, compassion, and grace to ourselves? Oftentimes, we do not. We need to be mindful of this, that all of humanity faces similar, yet different, challenges. One key area that I have learned to bring light to, is my own emotions and feelings, around certain things—to give them space to surface and work through them. If you are not willing to go there, you cannot heal—feelings buried alive, never die. It is time to name an area of struggle, where you wish to get traction and focus.

Your affirmation mantra is what you long for; it is going to become your reality, as you speak it out. Remember, healthy thoughts lead to healthy actions. Positive proclamations are your goal—no negative words! Personalize your affirmation mantra with an "I" or "my," as this exudes maximum power and makes it easy to remember, easy to repeat aloud. Take it even further: write it on your bathroom mirror and high five yourself every morning, as an added boost! Here are some samples:

> *"I believe in my skills and abilities to bring me a rich life."*
>
> *"I have the strength in me to create my success."*
>
> *"I naturally attract good fortune."*
>
> *"I control my money and my destiny."*
>
> *"Money flows easily to me and through me."*
>
> *"I give myself permission to prosper and grow abundantly."*
>
> *"I am open to give and receive; I am a money magnet."*

Now we are talking about money mantras and affirmations. I kid you not, we need mantras and affirmations, for all areas of our being. Do this same exercise for your self-worth, your identity, relationships, parenting, career, and spirituality. Each mantra will address an area of thought that needs to be dismantled and reframed. Until you reframe it, you will not be able to reposition yourself.

Play around; get a sense as to what resonates with your truth. How does your mantra feel in your body? Remember to always include your body, soul, and mind as one. Speak your mantra aloud to yourself, throughout the day: this is an added exercise to help it sink into your body.

To further this exercise I used a twelve-by-twelve piece of scrapbook paper and drew my head on it. Then, I grabbed a blue pen and wrote down all the lies that I believed, in bubbles around my head. This signified my thoughts—they were not pretty, let me tell you! Then, I had to dig deep and find the truth that canceled out each lie—that is what they were, and they snuck their way into my subconscious thoughts—through what I was told, learned, and experienced. I put my truths in red, bigger, so I would gravitate towards them. I then chose to dig deeper and decide when that lie first took root. What was the why behind it? I did this exercise and did not let it trigger me. I considered matter-of-fact, this happened. As a result, _____ is what I now believe.

You see, I was able to stay curious which kept shame and judgment at bay. You may recall me saying that curiosity is the antidote to judgement. I am extending grace, love, and acceptance, to the little girl within, that did the best that she could, while she was protecting me or keeping me safe. It's worth noting that no mantra will work without you doing the inner work alongside it. Just saying - there are no shortcuts.

This is so important to understand: that your fight, flight, freeze, or fawn response, does its best with the tools it has. When we enhance our knowledge and understanding, we have better tools available to work through these moments. This is growth, healing, and where your new story starts to take its shape, out of love. This exercise still sat beside my bed, even when my old programming tried to hijack my growth and healing. I was able to recognize, reflect, rebuke, reframe it, and hit the lie with these newfound truths. Along with breathing exercises, I was able to remain calm. Being proactive and not reactive with your healing journey, allows for you to reposition yourself and show up differently.

GETTING IN THE BODY EXERCISE

Here is a great exercise to take you out of your brain and into your body, for a second. Our minds and bodies must be able to communicate. The knowledge in your head needs to become heart understanding, to change your patterns and behaviors. Humor me, and try this exercise:

Stand tall and speak aloud your affirmation. Now slowly, vertebrae by vertebrae, starting with your head and neck, you will fold over, as if fingers are crawling down your spine. As you are doing this, whisper your mantra loudly. It should feel strange, as if it is coming from deeper inside you. Now do the same thing rolling back up, vertebrae by vertebrae, as you loudly whisper your mantra, continually. Repeat this, a couple of times once you reach the top. I wish for you to repeat your affirmation. This time, how did it sound? Was your voice different? Was it deeper, softer, higher, or lower? With practice, you will start to notice your voice shift and change, as you live out your truth. If you do not notice anything, that is okay, too—it took me a couple times, when I first did this exercise.

Each time you do it, you may notice a different word that grabs your attention. If you need to repeat only that word as you move vertebrae by vertebrae, do that. Your body will guide you on what is important. Then, reflect on why that phrase, word, even just the "I," had you. For me, one of my mantras is, "I am enough." I was stuck on the "am" for a while and finally when I was able to work through why that was so hard for me, I realized it stemmed from me believing, that if I say "I" or "am", that I was being selfish. Once I believed it in my heart, that "I am", my voice changed. My posture changed, the block between my head, and my heart, was gone, and I was able to live out my truth—that I *am* enough.

What is your truth? Identify your gap and address it with a plan.

Self-betrayal is acting in a way that is contrary to what you feel. When we betray ourselves, we see the world in a way that justifies our behavior and our self-betrayal. When we self-justify, our view of reality is distorted, and our mind becomes closed or we fall prey to "in the box" thinking.

Some character traits of "in the box" thinking are: inflating our faults, inflating our virtues, blaming, inflating the value of things that justify self-betrayal, seeing people as objects, and defensive posturing.

Challenges in today's culture that play a role: instant gratification, selfishness, entitlement, competing with others, disposable culture, lack of accountability, and family enabling.

Without a step forward, we remain in the same spot. So, why is it that we, as humans, self-sabotage our success? Out of fear, self-pity, self-justification, blame, or lack of confidence, we have been beaten down, so that we feel undeserving. The list can go on and on—trust me, I know.

It is one thing to experience fear of failure and fear of success, but our minds take it so much farther. Self-betrayal and self-sabotage happen, far too often, and this goes unchecked. Might I add that I know *why* it goes unchecked? It is challenging work to overcome!

How do we overcome both conscious and subconscious patterns? We evolve from being our greatest saboteurs, to becoming our own, biggest, cheerleaders.

READER REFLECTIONS

Repeat your money affirmation mantra.

What are your potential obstacles that may inhibit your affirmation?

How will you silence the noise from the world when it comes to the lies you believe about yourself and money?

What is your motivation, your WHY?

Empowerment time: where are your resources and how do you tap into them? (Think both internal and external resources.)

Chapter Seventeen: True North

"There is no way that a clear mind can live an unhappy life."

–Byron Katie.

Welcome to the chapter "True North," where we determine your future, where you wish to go, and where you see how far you have come. We will use the compass to break apart your stories into sections since when we categorize things, it can make it easier for us to look at them more matter-of-factly, which is what we want to do. Our focus is on the future, but what we have already gone through shapes us and warrants attention.

We all have a formula for success, and we've used it in the past, to get us through other things. We need to break apart the procedure, to apply it today. When we control our thoughts, we control our actions. Fear manifests in insecurity. Fear kills more dreams than failure ever will. So, instead of fear, we are looking for the formula for success.

I have done different exercises in hopes of renewing my mind; one being the thought bubble, with all the lies I believed about myself and my life. We need to get down to the foundation and build up, from there. When we do it, the kids can, and will, follow suit. Remember, you are a leader. No matter where you are in the world, others are watching you. I cannot stress the importance of your thoughts....affect your mental and physical health.

Life is a compass and True North is your future: It awaits you in complete alignment, and it operates from your most authentic, centered and wonderful self. You are purposeful and positioned to prosper. When we look back at the past, we turn our heads and look in the opposite direction, which is South.

South represents past experiences and learnings: So many of our beliefs are formulated here through our lenses, and you have carried them along for the ride.

Turn your attention to the East: this is where the sun rises, which signifies a new day, and a fresh start, full of possibilities. There is light, and where there is light, there is victory. The sun rises in the East and sets in the West.

The West signifies the end of something: The day has ended and there may have been adversities and challenges when you look West.

If you were to hold a compass in your hand, the North Star is always at the top, pointing forward. It is about positioning. You, in all actuality, may not be facing North, but you are facing forward. If you were to take steps forward, you would go somewhere. You can look in all directions: North, South, East and West, and every time you will return to True North, with the compass in your hand. With the north arrow you can see how perspective is everything. How you read a compass, matters. If you misread it, you will get lost. If you look back at your life and read it all wrong, you will get lost. But if you look back as if everything had a lesson, and a teachable moment, it would guide you to where you should go. You must trust your inner knowing and listen.

Focus on what is in front of you, not the left, right or behind you. This is your True North. Once we process our past, and heal, we can put our full attention on the future. That is why you hear me say, "True wealth starts within," as it frees you to reach wholeness, in all aspects of your life.

Navigating your story is not meant to relive the past. It is merely a way of recognizing what we were told and how we were treated. We have learned things, throughout our lifetimes, that have taken up real estate, in our minds. Our experiences and how we navigate them, are both good and bad. We discover learning and potential unlearning that has shaped our beliefs and programming. To dismantle these old narratives it requires unfolding your teachable moments. I say "teachable moments," as that is how we will use them. Together we will build the correct belief system that will empower you to flourish and thrive, regardless of the past narrative.

CORRECTING BELIEFS EXERCISE

Take inventory as to what is holding you back. This exercise may require a journal, giving you more room for reflection. Then, it will help to look at the lenses you have on and ask yourself some questions. These same questions lit a fire under me, so I will ask you the same:

What are the lies you believe about yourself that are holding you back?

Go deeper into the story, memory, or experience that brings this lie to life.

What were you told?

What did you learn, and from who/what?

What did you experience that contributed to this belief?

What will it cost you if you cannot overcome this old belief about yourself or others?

What are you most afraid of?

Where in your body does it reside?

If you see this through repeatedly, and you show up for yourself, you will become your best self for others.

We are building your compass, your True North, and achieving wholeness at a new level. We are reaching the core of who you are and what you were made to be. What is your "WHY?" Deep down, what do you want, and why do you want it? You are the author of your life, and it is time to rewrite your story as one of radiance, brilliance, and radical generosity. You, my friend, have a bigger game to play in the world. Your story is far too big to play a small game. Are you with me? Let us navigate South for a moment. Remember, we are not staying there to live it. Instead we are looking for teachable moments.

Reflect on your childhood, upbringing, education, training, career path, and professional history.

What roles have you played within your family or even your community? What lessons or learning can you take away or grow from?

Describe your most enjoyable life experience.

What made it enjoyable? What do you want more of?

Make note of these areas, so you know what fuels you and brings you joy. Better yet, make quadrants, like a compass. The first quadrant brings you joy and fuels your passion, and it would be best if you had this in your life. Stick with me, as we build out your formula.

What is your least enjoyable life experience?

What was going on, who was there, and what made it your least enjoyable?

Again, recognize if this shows up multiple times in your life and, if so, take inventory. This should go in the quadrant of "Hell No"—no more of that; it sucks the life out of me!

The other two quadrants are up for compromise, and you determine if you want more or less of them in your life. So, when you look at your life experiences and you think to yourself—"I need that in my life for purpose and joy," or "Hell, no! I do not want any part of that," —you are left with the following two:

> *It would be nice to have more of this in my life.*
>
> *This neither fuels me nor drains me—it's neutral.*

Take the time to unpack different life scenarios and how you contributed to your results.

For example, was there a lack of boundaries, or unhealthy beliefs about self, and others?

How were you treated by the most important people in your life, growing up?

What did you learn from them?

When you think about these people, how would they fit into your quadrants for your future self?

It is essential to surround yourself with people who fuel you and help you become better. Sometimes, in our lives we must cut toxic, draining people, out of our lives in order to establish healthy boundaries. Going through your memories and noting how others made you feel, will give you a good sense of who should stay, and who should go. Remember, you are the sum of the five people you spend the most time with—so choose wisely.

What did others say about you growing up? Good things, bad things? Think back to your relationships, parenting, and career. Are there lies you believe that you must recognize, reflect, rebuke, reframe, and reposition? I had to do this. Take it further; and ask yourself, "Who am I still harboring feelings toward? Are there people who need my forgiveness? Forgiveness is not for them; it is for you, to be free. Wholeness comes from freedom and letting go is a part of becoming your most authentic version. We can only tap into our compassion and forgiveness when we are operating from our aligned and emotionally regulated self.

We are shaking off all those negative thoughts just like a tree in the Fall sheds its leaves. It is time to release negative stored energy from your heart, mind, soul, and body. You want physical healing. There is truth to unforgiveness and how it shows up in one's body. Do your research, and you will see. You are digging deeper into your strengths and gifts to help determine your True North. What are you exceptional at doing? I am asking you to boast and brag without holding back. In contrast, others are not used to being in the spotlight and shining for all to see. It is your journal, so brag away.

What are three things that someone needs to know about you?

Are you living that out right now?

If so, great. If not, what can you do to make it true?

YOUR FORMULA FOR SUCCESS

Look back and see your track record of overcoming obstacles. If you did it then, you can do it now; the formula is already there. Where in your life have you had wins? Have they been in life, relationships, career, or business?

Tell me a story of what it was and how you went about achieving it.

If you journal it, (I hope you did), I want you to read your answers aloud. It helps you to metabolize it differently. If someone else had your story you would be inspired, proud of them, and happy for them. Give yourself that same praise—a job well done! So often, when faced with a new challenge or obstacle, we forget the last hurdles we were able to overcome. You are far more equipped now.

In what ways have you been innovative and creative and built new beginnings within your life? Funny story, my daughter tells me that when I stop being creative, I become a menace to society. She is right! Creativity is at the core of who I am. It makes me unique, authentic, vibrant, and fulfilled. Being creative expands our perceptions and enhances our problem-solving abilities. It is a superpower that makes life more fun, through improved brain function, and the ability to think outside the box.

Here is a list of what most people think of when they think of creativity:

- Art (painting/drawing, writing, singing/dancing, cooking, sewing/quilting/scrapbooking, redecorating, landscaping, designing, photography)

In addition to those amazing things, it is also:

- Switching perspectives, thinking outside the box, challenging the *status quo*, curiosity and possibility, building something, creating anything, finding a problem to solve, embracing differences, and being original.

How would creativity show up if you could bring creativity back into your life? We have transitions and/or endings throughout our lives, whether that is a dream that has transitioned, a relationship that ended, or a career that has shifted.

Where were your struggles and what did you consider to be failures?

Differentiate the "who" and "do". This was extensive learning for me, as I was in my kitchen in tears, when my marriage fell apart. My kids could not understand why I was crying so hard, and all I could muster was that I was a failure. I had believed the lie that I was a failure. That was who I was. They reminded me quickly that although I did fail, or fall, it was not "who" I was; instead, it was the "do" or "did." I learned that failing at a marriage was a 'do' not a 'who'. It helped me reposition myself out of victimhood and do better.

You have heard me say throughout this book: *Rethink Your Financial Health* that we have things within our control and out of our control. It is time we review them again. To do this, let us make it a practical application so you get more out of it.

What is one "top of mind" struggle that remains for you, as a person?

Can you spot saboteurs amid your battle? (Reference "Set Back to Set Up" Exercise)

What can you control given the circumstance or situation?

- Readiness: are you willing and able?

- Determination: do you have the required grit?

- Relationships with others: are you a helper or hinderer?

- Reactions and emotions: work through your emotions and how you respond.

- Radical responsibility: one hundred per cent accountability to yourself—show up and do better.

- Resourcefulness/collaboration: who can you pull in for help or expertise? We are never called to do things alone.

- Rest/balance: get sleep, eat well, exercise, and give your best to self and others.

- Alignment: bring your most authentic self to the table (emotionally regulated and centered.)

Throughout the last ten years, I have been told that what you fear, you create. If our minds are messy, our lives will be chaotic and our mental and physical health will, you guessed it, be dirty. I read the book *Cleaning Up Your Mental Mess,* by Dr. Caroline Leaf, and I loved it. She makes it simple, and it is backed by science.

Having a different view on worry, anxiety, and depression, was big for me as I was tired of watching, and having these labels placed on my loved ones, and even myself. So, here is my take on it: these are not labels that belong to us. They are, in fact, a warning signal for other things. And what is a warning? A warning is a signal that something needs to shift and change. When anxiety or depression surfaces, we need to spend time embracing, processing, and reconceptualizing life's sufferings and the pain we have endured. These feelings are intrinsically connected to our very own stories, where we are in the world, and our perceptual lenses, through which we view things. When we get these warning signs, we must uncover their valid message.

We all have stories and experiences which have created conscious and subconscious behaviors and beliefs. Through this narrative, we do life. We have a choice: we can be the architects of our brains and dismantle the old stories with great intentions. Now, when these uncomfortable emotions come up, instead of seeing them as unfavorable, hold curiosity. They may be telling you something about yourself that your mind and body have been covering up for years. Taking control of these emotions gives you the power to work *for* you, not *against* you. You are not celebrating the painful memories, you are conscious of them and what they mean, which plays a part in how you experience life today. Determine if you wish to carry it, or let it go.

Do you understand why we undergo emotions first, being able to label them, and apply the RULER approach? To think I learned about this in my forties, like, what? I give myself compassion, grace, and non-judgment. It is never too late to learn and grow.

I love the saying "What we water, grows." The same is true for our thoughts. What we pay attention to will only become magnified, which is why this chapter about our True North is so important. So many of us have thoughts that are not taking us in the direction we want to go. We need views that leverage us and align with our True North.

INTERTWINED EXERCISE

I am stoked to be making this journey with all of you. We will explore our minds and, of course our emotions. We covered that first, as it plays into all aspects. We will also bring awareness to our bodies and how this is all intertwined. In our minds, we can get stuck. We do not want to be frozen in time, yet often we end up that way. Then, we start to see the world through a different lens. Your life will always move in the direction of your most robust thoughts. What consumes your mind, controls your life. Live according to the know, believe, and do—this will help bring you into alignment and wholeness.

Know is head knowledge, believe is heart understanding, and with do, you get the actions needed.

Be determined to self-regulate your thinking, feeling, and choices. It is time to reboot your brain. Choose to not let any thoughts wander chaotically through your mind today. Catch them if they do, and RULER them out. Watch your words; what you speak is in your heart and mind. Words have the power to build or destroy. You have permission to feel, and you are, in fact, the creator of your own emotions, so manage them well.

Unpack any feelings that rear their ugly heads— forgiveness is critical.

Happiness hinges on what happens; seek joy.

Choose grace, compassion, and love for yourself and your journey.

Stay curious and kind, and lean in with possibilities, not limitations.

Hold a heart of gratitude.

You are designed for enhancement, not competition.

We are not called to do life alone—find a safe, authentic, faithful, and empowering support tribe.

READER REFLECTIONS

After doing an inventory, can you see gaps, or areas that need your attention?

"Those who turn good to great are motivated by a deep creative urge and an inner compulsion for sheer unadulterated excellence for its own sake. In contrast, those who build and perpetuate mediocrity are motivated more by fear of being left behind." –Good vs. Great Book.

You are now the director and designer of your life from this point forward. Congrats on owning this role! You now get to determine what stays and what goes, because you have built up these _____ (paradigms/boundaries/foundations). If one area does not serve you well, pitch it, rip out the page and just chuck it! The more aware you are of your thoughts and emotions, the more effective this process of rewriting your future will be.

What are you most excited about?

Chapter Eighteen: Communication - Yours Mine and Ours

"Attract what you expect, reflect what you desire, become what you respect, and mirror what you admire."

–Unknown.

As it turns out, my life is a guinea pig, in my line of work. I help people talk about money, emotions, and emotions around money, and I help them reach their financial finish lines. All of this came about organically, through my own life experience, and the challenges I faced in my relationships, when it came to the topic of money. I recently found this quote. If only I had found it sooner. This quote made me reflect on how I have lived out communication within relationships and money, back to the basics of doing unto others as you have them do unto you. Simple, timeless truths, yet hard to live by.

I talk about money stories, our old money narratives, and how we must dismantle subconscious patterns, to reach financial wholeness. I love what I do and spend my days helping people protect what is most important so they can live out their money differently. Now, I say this, because my now ex-husband, who listens to me prepare speeches and workshops, and is aware of my money workbook, completely caught me off guard when he purchased a truck, without discussing the matter. Oh yes, that happened! He went to the bank, got himself a line of credit, and decided to trade his current vehicle for a truck, without a word. This rocked me. Upon getting married the second time, we had full disclosure around money, and we agreed that any purchase above a thousand dollars would need to be discussed, prior. This slipped his mind and rational thinking went out the window, as he looked for a feel-good moment. This was an emotional purchase, and there was no communication regarding it. To this day it still is a sore spot for me. To be clear, I too, have a weakness regarding emotional purchases: puppies. So, a rule in our house was, if it could breathe it needs to be discussed as a family.

This segues into why communication in relationships is so important. I have interviewed many men and women regarding money, to get a feel for what works, and what does not. Others have shared that we all can use money to manipulate, control, power, numb, mask, and deflect. We do this both consciously and subconsciously. I will share that this experience with the truck sent me spiralling. I had a lot of work to go back to, when it came to my feelings of worthiness, identity, and career competence. Imposter syndrome was front and center.

Another person's actions had me activated and having to go back and do a lot of this work again and again. No one is immune.

The Four Lenses are applicable yet again:

What we were told.

What we learned.

What we experienced.

Most importantly, what we believe to be our truth comes from what we have lived out.

Based on these four lenses, we filter how we view money, life, relationships and communication.

Many of us have trauma associated with money, me included. That being said, having lost everything, and started over, money equals stability, to me. I want to know that I will be okay financially with no hidden surprises. So, I am returning to my money language of stability and scarcity mindset, after starting over. You can imagine that this truck purchase in a marriage, without communication would be viewed as "money infidelity". I joked about my books coming in from Amazon and hiding them on my bookshelf, feeling shame that I bought yet another one, when I have so many that I have not yet read. As my ex-husband would say, money infidelity is money infidelity, whether big or small. One gentleman laughed and said, "I hope it is a nice truck, nice enough for him to sleep in it!" I chuckled. Although we can all laugh at that, imagine how my ex feels now, with the shame, guilt, and judgment piling up. Money is a complex topic and comes with emotions. We need to work through them to get good with money.

I was shocked that something like this would happen to someone like me, who deals with money, and emotions, regularly. It sent me into a tailspin, thinking, "Am I a fraud, helping others with money, when I cannot even save my marriage?" That sounds about right; we can all feel like imposters. I had a lens I was looking through that was telling me a lie. I had to unpack it and work through it, allowing me to come to the other side and use the lessons as valuable teaching moments.

Why is this chapter so relevant in today's culture? This has led me to dig into what others say about money and communication. *Forbes* indicates that forty-five per cent of marriages end in divorce (I think it's higher), and financial stress plays a significant role in the deterioration of a relationship. However, in a survey of 1500 people, twenty per cent of participants manage their finances separately from their partners. Alarming, but wait, there is more:

- People are unsure if their partner has retirement savings.

- They do not know what their partner's credit score is.

- They do not share an account with a partner.

- They are unsure if the partner has debt.

- They are hesitant to share salary and financial information with a partner.

That same twenty per cent were experiencing money-related relationship problems—Hell ya, they would be!

Let's unpack that. When we carry so much shame, embarrassment, and guilt, it can feel challenging to discuss money topics. And, who goes first? I recall when I asked these questions in a previous relationship, and they were received poorly. Instead, I was labeled as controlling, micromanaging, and emasculating. That should have been my first indicator to run. I learned the hard way, lol. You may start over and ask yourself how you determine what yours, mine, and ours are. What are healthy money boundaries? How do you ask about the money side of life to a new partner or your significant other?

Here are a few questions you can start with:

- How do you manage your finances? Through Excel spreadsheets, on apps or paper?

- What were finances like in your previous relationship? Get specific, go back to the other chapters and if anything significant stood out, review this with your partner.

- What can we do differently, so as not to repeat previous money mistakes? Can we recognize the mistakes and label the underlying emotion, the root cause of the problem?

- What is your existing financial situation like? Be honest. Go back to the quote that opened this chapter.

- Will we merge accounts and assets? Prenuptial agreements: there is no right or wrong, when talking openly allows for realistic expectations.

- Who is responsible for the cost of running a home?

- What level of support for additional children outside and inside the home is needed?

- Are there financial obligations in place prior to this relationship? For example, child and spousal support agreements.

- How would you like to see your finances played out?

- What fears do you have concerning money?

Here is my take: you should know one another's debts, interest rates, account balances, investments, and returns on investments. There should be a goal for when a debt should be reduced to zero—a game plan if you wish. It would be best if you only take on additional debt, after discussing it. Remember, debt mortgages your future. For example, if you take on a new vehicle loan something may come up later that you may need to say no to. Debt changes your standard of living in the future, until it is paid off.

Here are questions you can ask yourself before making a large purchase:

- What is driving this decision?

- Are there emotions attached?

- Is it a want, like, love, or need?

- Is my partner included? Are we aligned?

- What is your maximum purchase without a discussion?

- What will the entire cost of a purchase be, with interest? Know what exactly you will be paying for something.

- Talk about having two accounts, one combined and one separate (everyone needs a little money of their own, with transparency).

- Discussing and establishing a goal and working towards it is essential. Having a budget/spending plan, paying bills, reducing debt, and building a margin for your future are critical to relationship success.

- Finally, there needs to be room for autonomy. Too much restriction can cause resentment, secrecy, control, or manipulation. Make vision boards as a couple, and separate vision boards for yourself, even involve your kids to do a family money vision board!

I like what Holly Trantham says:

> Financial compatibility does not mean you need to go looking for a partner with the same financial standing as yourself—or that you need to kick someone to the curb because they don't earn enough money. Rather, this compatibility has much more to do with your respective attitudes and habits surrounding money.

I like that. Fixed mindset or growth mindset. These words keep coming to me: stay curious and lean in with possibility. This stuff is not taught in school, or often, even at home. Remember, money, "back in the day," was often a taboo topic. So, we learned from what we were told, an experience that led us to behave in certain ways, regarding money and relationships.

Here is where I am challenging us collectively to reflect on what lenses we may have, regarding our communication around money. "For me, this is what my money looks like": go first; start the conversation. Be transparent; remember omitting is no different than lying. And nothing is worse than having to ask question after question. Come to the conversation with full disclosure. More is always better than letting the other person try to guess or ask more questions. You will need to check your ego, pride, shame, guilt, and embarrassment, at the door. These are my money goals: be specific, concise, and share your "why", because that is what drives you. It should mean something to your partner if it means something to you.

Next, make a quadrant list of your combined goals. I use this method for everything in life.

- Highest priority next five years.

- It would be a nice bonus.

- I can wait, but within ten years.

- I am letting it go.

What would combining finances look like? Here is the reality, even if you and your partner do not combine finances anytime soon, or ever—their money situation will affect yours always and vice versa. *Know before you go, ha-ha.* Back in the day, when you married your high school sweetheart, or built everything from the ground up together, fewer blended families were navigating "yours, mine, and ours." Be intentional and purposeful. Knowing or having an idea of how you will manage finances through different transitions with a blended family, is essential.

Other topics for discussion are as follows:

- Is there an allowance?

- What does phone accountability look like?

- Kids' braces, will you share the load?

- Kids' first vehicle, who is responsible?

- Will you pay for secondary education? How much?

- Boundaries when kids need help.

- If you do for one, do you do for all? For example, what side of the fence do you and your partner sit on?

- When is it helping and when is it enabling? How will that be played out if an adult child needs financial help?

- How will we protect the kids/grandkids with insurance, or do we?

- What do spousal payments or child payments look like?

- Where will that money go when it has all done?

I love the idea of a shared vision board for the new family. Teach young and old kids that communication about money is normal and healthy in relationships. They will follow suit in their relationships, later in life. Remember, kids are watching if the vision board has financial goals and dreams, then it also makes it easier to say no to things and reference the board. Sound financial decisions take intention, sacrifice, and planning. They, too, have the vision; they will carry that forward, later in life.

Never fight about money in front of kids; here is a better tip given to me when I interviewed a man. He informed me that he and his wife talked about money in the car. I was intrigued and asked him to tell me more. He said that kids listen when they are in the back seat; what a perfect time to rationally discuss money, goals, objectives, and boundaries, so the kids subconsciously take it in. How clever! I wish I had thought of that. We all have nuggets of wisdom that need to be shared. Talking in the car is now one of my tactics to have a complicated discussion, as no one can get away, especially at high speeds!

Our relationship with money is complex. There are challenges and opportunities, where we make financial decisions. These decisions affect our feelings and future behaviors, and they are constantly evolving. Emotions play a huge role in anxiety, and avoidance keeps you in the same cycle. Pay attention to these emotions, as they tend to override your rational thinking: fear, guilt, shame, and envy. For example, my ex-husband experienced envy of others having a better vehicle than him, paired with the embarrassment of having to start financially over after his divorce. He, too, had some entitlement there, as he was the primary income-earner, and wanted to feel better about himself. Apparently, he thought a big purchase would do the trick. You see, his emotions overtook his rational thinking! I like what Prudy Gourguechon says:

> Shame interacts with avoidance to create a vicious cycle. When you are filled with shame, you avoid the conversation entirely as it is uncomfortable. Conversely, avoidance reduces anxiety - hence why so many fall into it, but this sabotages your financial future, leaves you stuck, and hurts relationships due to a lack of trust.

Much of our emotional world is unconscious. Establishing proper communication with your partner, you can establish a blueprint for emotions, behaviors, and money stories that can positively influence your relationship with money. This will help you reach wholeness, a thriving marriage, and thriving finances.

I often talk about head knowledge becoming heart understanding, so you can live it out. Now it is time for application: how do you start the difficult conversations, so they can become head and heart, for both parties?

TALK MONEY HONEY EXERCISE

Here is how to start talking money with your partner. It takes less than fifteen minutes per week. You will need these materials:

- Sticky notes in two distinct colors.

- Pens.

- A small storage box.

Considering the stats are high for divorce, and one of the top reasons has to do with money, we can stand to follow sage tips to give ourselves a fighting chance. Starting over with someone is effing hard in all areas, especially money. Different patterns, behaviors, money stories, traumas, and superiority complexes do not make this easy. Here is a solid starting point. It opens the door softly, allowing you to build your skills and communication styles:

- Each person writes on their sticky note what they did well with money this week.

- On the second sticky note, you write down what you did poorly with money this week.

- Third, each write what you want to do better with money next week and how you will do it.

- Share. No comments, no judgment, or helping the other person do theirs.

- Save these sticky notes and do this exercise every week.

Remember this exercise should take you at most, ten minutes. Itis about personal reflection, ownership, and self-accountability. After that, you will begin to see your patterns. Then, at the end of the month, each of you takes personal time to dig deep into why you have that pattern. What is the root cause and the story underneath? Then, it is time to dismantle it.

Once this exercise is mastered as a couple, try adding this next one:

Monthly Money Date Night: At the end of every month, tally up your outgoing expenses against what is coming in. Is there a surplus (in the black/extra money after all obligations are met) or a deficit (in the red/spending more than you make)?

If there is a surplus, allocate that money. You can spend a little or put it towards your goals. Establish both short-term and long-term goals as a couple.

If there is a deficit, pull out your sticky notes. How can you make changes? Again, no judgment, no condemning—know better, do better.

You need to pay attention to emotions like fear, guilt, shame, and envy, as they tend to override your rational thinking. When we apply the knowledge we just learned, results happen and mindsets shift. Eventually these minor changes become significant changes.

READER REFLECTIONS

What are your next steps? Journal or write down what you wish to implement and list a due date. Send a text to your partner and mention this incredible exercise that you want to do that takes less than ten minutes and will help with money communication!

What questions have you already asked, and which ones do you need to learn more about with your partner?

When there are specific questions that make you anxious to discuss, ask yourself why and what could be behind that. It is a fantastic way to start the work before doing it jointly, as each of us has junk in our trunk regarding past relationships and money.

Lean in with curiosity and possibility. Then, go back to the quote that opened this chapter and press in. "Attract what you expect, reflect what you desire, become what you respect, and mirror what you admire." –Unknown.

Chapter Nineteen:
Money Quadrants

"Money is a tool that will take you wherever you wish. But it will not replace you as the driver."

–Ayn Rand.

Let us start with the definition of contentment (noun): a state of happiness and satisfaction. Contentment is a choice!

It is important to remember this when we think about money, our future, the decisions we make, and why we are making them. Understanding the four uses of money by Mr. Ron Blue's *Live, Give, Owe, Grow*, along with what I refer to as the money quadrants: *Like, Love, Need, Want.* Pair it with emotional intelligence and you have financial confidence. Those who manage their money using both concepts experience contentment under all economic conditions. Increased communication, unity within partnerships, maximizing generosity of time and money. Our aim is financial wholeness and a life of significance: it happens here. I love quadrants, and I use them for most things in life, as they bring clarity to situations. The four uses of money:

Live: Spend less than you earn and live within your means. But, first, determine what your "enough" is.

Give: Give to causes that stir your heart. Giving back breaks the power that money can have on us and efficiently reduces our taxes. Giving can be monetary and non-monetary, such as your time, talent, and gifts.

Owe: Pay off your debt, pay what you owe, avoid using debt, and pay your taxes as it is a sign of provision.

Grow: Create margins to meet your goals, save for your future income needs, and align your investments to your values.

What you water, grows. If you water your lifestyle, it will increase in cost. If you water your savings, they too will prosper. Put thought into what you are watering. If you grow your debt, you will be drowning soon. The same is true for your thoughts. Now here are the quadrants:

Need: What does it mean to need something? These would be your essentials, your necessities. You cannot do life without these: food, shelter, education, and insurance.

Love: How to determine if it is a love or like? Here is how: ask if it will bring you joy <u>longer than six months.</u> Ask yourself if it will bring joy to others, for an extended amount of time. Sustainability?

Like: What is driving this desire? Is it an emotion? Typically, to "have," will only bring joy for a limited amount of time—<u>less than six months</u>. So, when you say yes to something today, it means you have to say no to something, often in the future.

Want: Be cautious here. A want is typically driven by emotion, something fleeting, instant gratification, only a band-aid to what is going on underneath. It is a temporary pleasure that dies off quickly, leaving you with shame, guilt, and remorse. Are you doing it to feel good, numb a feeling, mask, or cover something up, or be jealous? The list is long.

I am giving you the key to success with the following skills that you should master:

Decision Making

- What is driving you and the financial decision that you are making?

- There is no independent financial decision.

- Advance lifestyle decision-making bears fruit that carries on for generations and creates freedom.

Goal Setting

- Set both short-term and long-term goals for your future.

- Celebrate the wins.

- Sacrifice is always a trade-off.

- Accountability leads to peace of mind.

- Meaningful life-planning legacy, by design, or default—the choice is yours.

Cash Flow Management

- The longer term your perspective, the better your financial decision today.

- Debt mortgages your future.

- Financial maturity is being able to give up today's desires for future benefits.

Wealth Transfer

- Pass along morals, values, and wisdom before money.

- Training the next generation to manage money has the by-product of character development.

- Teaching the head is training to the heart; more is caught than taught.

- A trade-off between time and effort, money, and rewards.

- Notice your past financial decisions; which quadrants do they fall into?

- Need, Like, Love, or Want

MASTER YOUR MONEY EXERCISE

How did the lenses of what you were told, learned, experienced, and believed to be true, play out with how you categorize essential things?
What do you think about contentment?
What filters do you need to dismantle and reframe so you can reposition yourself better for your future?
Was there an emotion or feeling that drove your purchase?
How can you set yourself up in the future to be more conscious about emotions and money?

All these are helpful tips, but if you still have lenses that you are viewing money through that are unhealthy— you need to take the time to dismantle them and what lies beneath. I will repeat the R's here, for you to work through the beliefs limiting your success.

Recognize: what is happening and how it is showing up in your finances.

Reflect: on where it came from in your life using your lenses.

Rebuke: determine that it is a lie and has no power over you.

Reframe: what is your truth? Where do you see the future that you dream of being?

Reposition: take that truth and "be it till you become it." Live out differently.

As you work through the R's, you can take your head knowledge and shift it down to your heart understanding. Believe that more is possible for your life and live out that desire. Fuel the momentum you get from the desire to be and get to the core of your why. Why is this future important? Create an action plan to get there.

Break it down to bite size pieces.

- 30-day plan

- 60-day plan

- 90-day plan

- 180-day plan

READER REFLECTIONS

Having a plan of action is where the rubber meets the road; hold yourself accountable to make the changes necessary to reach your financial finish lines. Start checking things off, and when you find yourself procrastinating—which will happen, life gets busy, and you get distracted—ask yourself what it costs you *not* to live out the most authentic version of yourself.

Chapter Twenty:
Connecting the Dots

"Too many people spend money they don't have to buy things they don't need, to impress people they don't even like."

–Will Rogers.

In life, we have choices. We can dictate, or we can model a particular behavior. I remember being challenged by discipline for my kids, then I listened to a podcast that changed my perspective on parenting. The origin of the word "discipline", is from a disciple, modelling a particular way of living. That is what we are called to do, as humans, in this life. To live out the best we can, with the knowledge and wisdom given to us. Lead the way, so others can follow. Think of yourself as the thermostat to the house: if you are grumpy, guess what? The whole damn house will be moody, soon! If you are happy, everyone else tends to jump on that bandwagon.

When it comes to emotional intelligence, it must start somewhere, so why not build up yours today and let the results trickle down to others within your circle of influence? When we get good with emotions, we can better oversee life, relationships, parenting, careers, and finances. We can self-regulate and take ourselves out of the nervous system responses of fight, flight, freeze, and fawn. Understanding that if we choose not to build up our emotional toolbox, we rob ourselves of the best life possible.

So much of this work starts within. That is why I have called your financial health a healing journey, because it is. So much of our lives we have lived things out, not because they *are* true but because we *believe* them to be true. There is a significant difference.

Last time to hit these lenses and drive them home:

What Were We Told? What are the things we were told about ourselves, others, the environment, society, relationships, money, and so much more?

What Did We Learn? We pick things up through our senses. What did we see, hear, taste, smell, and touch that made an imprint on us?

What Did We Experience? Events in our lives can significantly impact how we live out; they can be their own belief system or add to what you have already been told. This will only solidify what you believe to be true, even though it may not be.

What Do We Believe? We need to remember that in life, we create a story from all these lenses, and then we live out looking for the proof, facts, and things to validate what we believe already.

Here is a light and funny example my kids consistently demonstrate: "He doesn't even care about me." My son chose not to go to his sister's volleyball game and suddenly she is crying, saying, "he does not even care about me." I ask her what is making her feel this way? "He doesn't like my music, judges my food choices, and makes fun of me all the time." Now, I know you may all be like, "regular activities between siblings," and while yes, this behaviour is expected, we must ask ourselves what messages we are giving that contribute to the story. So here, she created this story that "no one cares" about her. She has found multiple things she heard, saw, or experienced, that allowed her to believe her own story and validate it. This was not the case. Though there were conflicting schedules, he could not make it. He was recommending different music, and she took it that he did not like hers; he mentioned another snack option, and she felt judged. Even a little teasing was taken to the extreme.

Are these feelings valid? One hundred per cent. No one can tell us how to feel. We need to reach what may be under the emotion and see what lenses we are looking through. Is it true, or are we running a story that needs correcting? When we feel intense emotions, our natural response is to do something that makes us feel better. Naturally, my daughter gravitates to eating, scrolling on social media, or online shopping like her mom—she learned it from me.

Can you see how these patterns play into our partners' lives, friends, family, kids, and community? It is all intertwined and affects all areas: physical health, mental health, emotional health, and financial health. It starts with you, to make the changes in yourself first, so others within your close circle can follow suit.

RUBBER MEETS THE ROAD EXERCISE

KNOW is head knowledge.

- Understand the working of your spending habits and decision-making regarding finances.

- What are the stories that you have scripted in your mind?

- Know your finances inside and out!

- Work through your money languages to bring about self-reflection and marital unity.

- Establish your finish lines, and articulate where you are going, and why.

- Roadmap to get you there—who is helping you?

- What are your TOP priority improvement goals?

BELIEVE is heart understanding.

- What is important to YOU, and why?

- What are you most afraid of?

- What keeps you up at night?

- How does your heart feel, knowing your current financial situation?

- How will your heart feel upon reaching your finish lines?

- What change do you want to see in the world?

- What behaviors do you have that sabotage your success?

- How does that make you feel?

- What has more value, return on investment, or return on life?

- What is stopping you from achieving your goals?

DO is choosing to live differently.

- The mind and heart will propel you forward to reach your goals.

- Actions without work are dead. Rubber meets the road when you implement the plan.

- Sacrifice leads to sound financial decisions.

- When you know better, you do better; this is transformative.

- Overcome your assumptions and stories— replace them with the truth.

- You have hope and a future, and YOU GOT THIS!

READER REFLECTION

Inventory Time:

1. Think about the things you have been told, learned, and experienced. What have you believed to be valid from all those lenses? Our beliefs lead to thoughts. Thoughts lead to actions, and actions to behaviors. Is how you are living out right now bringing you closer to wholeness, or distancing you, and keeping you stuck?

2. Read this quote and then ask yourself, do you need to feel psychologically safe and build up your emotional intelligence? (I know I did; the kids and I started this journey back in 2000) "When children learn in psychologically safe environments that nurture their emotional skills, can they move from helplessness to resilience, from anxiety to action, from scattered to centered, from isolated to connected." –Mark Brackett.

3. What is possible, if you can gain traction, and release your old narratives? Close your eyes and envision your future self. It may take a bit, but let images and senses flood your mind. How does it feel in your body? What is the feeling this gives you? Do you know where you are? What are you doing? Who is around you? Now journal your findings and be open to receiving this future version of yourself.

4. How has working through all of this made you feel? What did you experience, and where did resistance show up for you? Were you able to get to the root of the opposition? Remember Brene Brown's quote, "Integrity is choosing courage over comfort. It's choosing what's right over what is fun, fast, or easy, and practicing your values, not just professing them."

5. In all areas, you have a choice: will you show up for yourself and your future and do the work? You are the author of your life. You determine the chapters and can rewrite your story into one of radiance, brilliance, and radical generosity. You, my friend, have a bigger game to play in this world. Your story is far too big to play a small game! The choice is yours.

6. Did you make a money mantra? If not, ask yourself, "Why not?" There might be something under that. If you did, where did you put it? Be sure to change it and move it around.

7. Do you want GOOD or GREAT? Jim Collins says, "Those who turn good to great are motivated by a deep creative urge and an inner compulsion for sheer unadulterated excellence for its own sake. In contrast, those who build and perpetuate mediocrity are motivated more by fear or being left behind." Now, which are YOU?

8. Do you feel shame, guilt, embarrassment, or judgment? Can you bring it to the light? Start with awareness, acknowledgement, self-reflection, and radical responsibility. Work through it, my dear ones. Ask yourself, is it misplaced guilt, shame, or embarrassment?

9. What will it cost you if you do not change your financial health? Are you willing to live with that cost? If not, take steps to break free from it, as financial freedom is there for the taking.

10. What are you most afraid of? Let us discuss that ONE! Do something today that your future self will thank you for.

Find the true story that holds your power within, that, my dear ones, is your superpower.

"If you can't control your emotions, you cannot control your money." –Warren Buffett.

Congratulations on putting your financial health front and center; I hope this book can release the old money story that wasn't serving you well and embark on this new you that will have your finances shifting in no time flat.

Doing the work was not an easy task or journey for me, and I know that you, too, have put some of your sweat, laughter, and tears into the exercises throughout this book: Rethink Your Financial Health.

I hope you found this book thought-provoking and life changing as you unlearn and relearn what it means to be financially whole and healthy.

Rethink your financial health through the lenses:

What you were told.

What you learned.

What you experienced.

What you believed to be your truth.

Brings healing to what you have believed about your self-worth, identity, the world, communication, money, security, love for self and others, and so much more.

The work doesn't stop here, my friends. You can take it further with the Financial Scorecard on the following pages.

Thank you for reading this book and putting yourself first. For all your hard work I would like to offer you a complimentary money coaching session to dive into the areas you still may face resistance.

It is time we view money as more than numbers. Money affects all areas of our lives, and we must lead the way for the next generation.

Pass the baton!

Financial Health Scorecard

I love this scorecard, as it gives you an idea of areas you can strengthen, and at what you are rocking. Then, you can build out a plan to increase and enhance your overall financial health, in the other areas.

PROGRESS OVER PERFECTION-this will change your inner perfectionist, as I experienced.

aj *sharing the manual*

THIS IS YOUR
FINANCIAL HEALTH

scorecard

Sharing the manual

Financial Health Scorecard

↘ ASSESS YOUR FINANCIAL HEALTH

Complete the questions using PART 2 of the pie diagram. Be truthful, have no judgement, and hold space for curiosity as it is the antidote. What could be underneath? We can then dive deeper into what lens you created this narrative behind and dismantle it so you can flourish and thrive financially. A score between 0-10, zero on the low end, ten means you are kicking ass.

PART 1 ✕

☐ **empowered**
Do you feel empowered by your current financial situation?

☐ **awareness**
Are you self-aware of your money patterns and behaviours?

☐ **communication**
Can you communicate effectively with your partner about money?

☐ **confidence**
Are you confident about your financial future?
I have a plan in place to reach my financial goals.

☐ **entrepenueral**
Do you have multiple streams of income? Are you a go-getter?

☐ **growth mindset**
Are you able to learn and grow from your past money mistakes?
Are you continually learning?
Always looking to grow your financial literacy.

☐ **accountability**
I take 100% responsibility for my current financial situation?

☐ **emotional intelligence**
Are you able to recognize when emotions are driving your purchases?

Financial Health Scorecard

PART 2

Using a scale of 0 -10, zero being low awareness and ten being a rockstar. Place a dot on the line representing you and where you are today in each category. Then connect your dots to see the complete picture. Finally, book your 60-minute complimentary coaching session for tips and tricks to enhance your financial health.

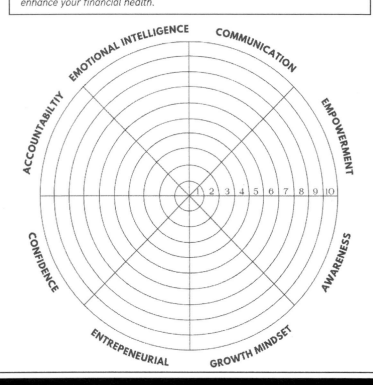

Financial Health Scorecard

Complete the questions using PART 4 of the pie diagram. Be truthful, have no judgement, and hold space for curiosity as it is the antidote. What could be underneath? We can then dive deeper into what lens you created this narrative behind and dismantle it so you can flourish and thrive financially. A score between 0-10, zero on the low end, ten means you are kicking ass.

PART 3

☐ **beliefs**
Do your current money beliefs allow you to flourish?

☐ **mindfulness**
Are your thoughts about finances positioning you to thrive?

☐ **physical symptoms**
Are you able to regulate financial stress in the body?

☐ **emotions**
Are you able to control your emotions prior to spending?
Can you self regulate?

☐ **spiritual**
Do your spiritual beliefs align with your spending habits?

☐ **giving back**
Are you giving back in a way that brings abundance and opportunity for others?

☐ **career**
Is your current career allowing you to thrive financially?
Are you making what you are worth?

☐ **relationships**
Are you in a relationship that builds positivity with your money?
Does your existing community affect your finances?

Financial Health Scorecard

PART 4

Using a scale of 0 -10, zero being low awareness and ten being a rockstar. Place a dot on the line representing you and where you are today in each category. Then connect your dots to see the complete picture. Finally, book your 60-minute complimentary coaching session for tips and tricks to enhance your financial health.

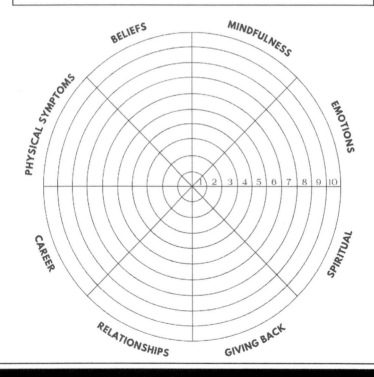

Self Reflection

JOURNAL YOUR THOUGHTS AND FEELINGS.
WHERE ARE YOUR STRENGTHS AND WEAKNESSES?

What Surprised You? ✕

↘ Key Notes

Next Steps →

↘ WHAT ARE YOUR MOST CRITICAL AREAS FOR GROWTH?

Choose two areas you'd like to work on over the next few months. Write down a SMART goal for each of them. Finally, list any actions you need to achieve your goals.

Come as you are...

We take you deeper through the process - SERVING YOU IN ANY STAGE.

In addition to our Financial Wholeness Ten-Week 1:1 Coaching Package & Workbook we offer the following services:

- build out a money roadmap that reaches your finish lines
- workshops / webinars
- key note speaking/conferences/events
- money coaching individual and group sessions
- financial healing journey
- budgeting - cash flow analysis
- net worth summary
- savings regimen
- insurance products
- investment products
- sounding board
- second opinion
- referral to a professional advisory team of lawyers or accountants
- problem-solving - solutions driven
- full gamut: determining your finish lines and creating a custom plan, implementation, continual review

Reach out at amie@sharingthemanual.ca - 403-866-5600 - www.sharingthemanual.ca

connecting the dots

you should connect

REFERENCES

Chapter Two
"Money mindset is a unique set of beliefs and your attitude about money." Ramsey, D (2007). The Total Money Makeover: A Proven Plan for Financial Fitness. Thomas Nelson Inc.

Chapter Three
Aliche, T. (2022). **Financial Wholeness is when all aspects of your financial life are working together for your greatest good, your biggest benefit, and your richest life.**
https://getgoodwithmoney.com/

Rand. A. (2022) **Money is only a tool. It will take you wherever you wish. But it will not replace you as the driver.**
https://www.brainyquote.com/quotes/ayn_rand_124992

Chapter Seven
"It is your job to disappoint as many people as possible as long as you do not disappoint yourself." Doyle, G. (2020). Untamed. The Dial Press, an imprint of Random House, a division of Penguin Random House LLC.

"Healing cannot occur if we do not accept our worthiness-that we are worth healing, even if doing so might shake up our view of the world and how we interact with others."

Mario Martinez Gabor, M. (2022). The Myth of Normal. Penguin Random House

Chapter Nine
Tessler, B. (2022) **"We can't think our way out of feelings! The best we can do is say hello to them, calm ourselves down, and stay gentle with ourselves as we allow our feelings to move through."** https://baritessler.com/
Katie, B. (2022) **"Byron Katie's four questions."** https://theageofideas.com/byron-katies-four-questions/

Wellness Innovate Corp. (2021) Certified Flourishing Coaching. "Obstacles and Controllables" & "True North Compass"

Crary, M. (2012) **"How Being a Control Freak About Money Blocks Intimacy"** Forbes Article. https://www.forbes.com/sites/moneywisewomen/2012/06/11/how-being-a-control-freak-blocks-intimacy-money/?sh=719a55c07b9c

Evans, B. (2019). **"Decide whether to quit, pivot, or persevere. Learn how to quit well. Get to grips with the diverse ways to pivot. Build passion and perseverance to grow."** How To Have a Happy Hustle. Icon Books Ltd.

Plett. H. (2020) **"We slowly but surely lose touch with our identity. We lose our free spirit, our uniqueness, and our authenticity. By careful imitation, punishment, and shaming, we learn how to survive the environment into which we were born. We take our wildness, our nonconformity, and our defiance. We put on masks to hide aspects of ourselves that we believe are unacceptable to the world. We become people our parents, teachers, and other influencers expect us to be. We learn to fit the culture."** The Art of Holding Space. Page Two Books Inc.

Chapter Thirteen

Elwaynes, C.B. **"Red light, green light, and centred concepts."** Bold & Visible Program (2022)

Warren, S. (2022) **"Body Postures: Red Light, Green Light, and Centred"** https://somaticmovementcenter.com/

Chapter Fourteen

Chapman, G. (1992). **"The Five Love Languages".** The Five Love Languages: The Secret to Love That Lasts. Northfield Publishing

Dowell, C. (2017) **"The Wealth Languages or Money Languages"** The Wealth Languages. Kingdom Advisors

Brown, B. (2017). **"The story I am telling myself is…"** Rising Strong: How the Ability to Reset Transforms the Way We Live, Love, Parent, and Lead. Random House

Chapter Eighteen

Trantham, H. (2018) **"Financial compatibility does not mean you need to go looking for a partner with the same financial standing as yourself - or that you need to kick someone to the curb because they don't earn enough money. Rather, this compatibility has much more to do with your respective attitudes and habits surrounding money."** Better by Today Article https://www.nbcnews.com/better/business/3-money-conversations-you-your-partner-need-have-ncna846016

Gourguechon, P. (2019) **"Shame interacts with avoidance to create a vicious cycle. When you are filled with shame, you avoid the conversation entirely as it is uncomfortable. Conversely, avoidance reduces anxiety - hence why so many fall into it, but this sabotages your financial**

future, leaves you stuck, and hurts relationships due to a lack of trust." Forbes Article. https://www.forbes.com/sites/prudygourguechon/2019/02/25/the-psychology-of-money-what-you-need-to-know-to-have-a-relatively-fearless-financial-life/?sh=5a92fb4adfe8

Dorsainvil, Rianka. (2019) **"Why Communicating About Money is Key to a Healthy Relationship and Financial Future"** Forbes Article. https://www.forbes.com/sites/riankadorsainvil/2019/08/28/why-communicating-about-money-is-key-to-a-healthy-relationship-and-financial-future/?sh=5171df39749b

Chapter Nineteen
Blue, R. (2013). **"LIVE, GIVE, OWE, GROW Money Concept"** Kingdom Advisors. Ron Blue Institute. https://ronblueinstitute.com/

Chapter Twenty
Brackett, M. (2019) **"When children learn in psychologically safe environments that nurture their emotional skills, can they move from helplessness to resilience, from anxiety to action, from scattered to centered, from isolated to connected."** *Permission to Feel*: Unlocking the Power of Emotions to Help Our Kids, Ourselves, and Our Society Thrive. Celadon Books

Collins, J. (2001) **"Those who turn good to great are motivated by a deep creative urge and an inner compulsion for sheer unadulterated excellence for its own sake. In contrast, those who build and perpetuate mediocrity are motivated more by fear or being left behind."** Good to Great: Why Some Companies Make the Leap...and Others Don't. Harper Collins Publishers.

RECOMMENDED READING

The Body Keeps the Score: Brain, Mind, And Body In The Healing of Trauma. by Van Der Kolk, MD. B (2015). Viking Penguin.

The High 5 Habit by Robbins, M. (2021). Hay House.

Happy Days: The Guided Path from Trauma to Profound Freedom and Inner Peace by Bernstein, G. (2022). Hay House

Immunity To Change: How to Overcome It and Unlock the Potential In Yourself and Your Organization by Kegan, R and Laskow Lahey, L. (2009). Harvard Business School Publishing Corporation.

No Bad Parts: Healing Trauma & Restoring Wholeness with The Internal Family Systems Model by Schwartz, R. C. (2021). Sounds True Inc.

Permission to Feel: Unlocking the Power of Emotions to Help Our Kids, Ourselves, and Our Society Thrive. Brackett, M. (2019). Celadon Books Publisher.

Anchored: How to Befriend Your Nervous System Using Polyvagal Theory. Dana, D. (2021). Sounds True.

Cleaning Up Your Mental Mess: 5 Simple, Scientifically Proven Steps to Reduce Anxiety, Stress, and Toxic Thinking. Leaf, C. (2021). Baker Books